To Mr. Gun,

The only person I know who was related to a "Polar Bear." Enjoy the book!

Lorraine ☺

10.19.02

THE UNITED STATES INTERVENTION IN NORTH RUSSIA–1918, 1919

THE UNITED STATES INTERVENTION IN NORTH RUSSIA–1918, 1919
The Polar Bear Odyssey

Roger Crownover

The Edwin Mellen Press
Lewiston•Queenston•Lampeter

Library of Congress Cataloging-in-Publication Data

Crownover, Roger.
   The United States intervention in North Russia, 1918, 1919 : the Polar Bear odyssey /
Roger Crownover.
      p. cm.
   Includes bibliographical references and index.
   ISBN 0-7734-7549-4
      1. Soviet Union--History--Allied intervention, 1918-1920. 2. Soviet
Union--History--Revolution, 1917-1921--Participation, American. 3. United States.
Army. Infantry, 339th--History. I. Title.

   DK265.42.U5 C76 2001
   947.084'1--dc21

                                                                    00-048114

A CIP catalog record for this book is available from the British Library.

Front Cover: The Day the Polar Bears Came Home, July 4, 1919.
Marching Down Central Avenue, on Belle Isle, Detroit, Michigan.

         The Edwin Mellen Press   The Edwin Mellen Press
               Box 450   Box 67
         Lewiston, New York   Queenston, Ontario
         USA 14092-0450   CANADA L0S 1L0

                     The Edwin Mellen Press, Ltd.
                     Lampeter, Ceredigion, Wales
                     UNITED KINGDOM SA48 8LT

                Printed in the United States of America

To those who have enriched my life:
My parents, William and Mary Crownover
My wife, Chris
My children, Scott and Joyelle

CONTENTS

PROLOGUE

FOUR LEAF CLOVER: THE POLAR BEAR ODYSSEY
The United States Intervention in North Russia 1918-1919

The year was 1918. The event was the end of World War I. The locale was Russia. The participants were American soldiers (with other Allied forces), the Bolshevik Red Army, and the Russian White Army. The conflict was the fighting among all three armies. World War I ended in November of 1918 but some Americans were ordered to continue to fight and die for an unknown reason in that far away country. The American soldiers complained bitterly about a number of areas: they felt mistreated by their British superiors, they were not told why they were to continue to fight after the Armistice, they felt their British counterparts were given special treatment, and most importantly, they felt abandoned by their own government.

This historical fact, that took place seventy-seven years ago, is not well known by the general public and seldom mentioned in American history books. Many Americans are astonished when told that the United States sent armed troops to Russia near the end of World War I to fight the Russian Bolsheviks. Russian students have always been taught about this incident. This group of American men were officially known as the North Russian Expeditionary Forces, or better known as the "Polar Bears." The Detroit newspapers called them "Detroit's Own." The majority of the 5,500 Americans were from Michigan. They were trained (some for as little as three weeks) at Camp Custer, Battle Creek, Michigan and sent to New York, then to England, and finally arrived in Russia.

i

What not only makes this event unusual, besides fighting on Russian soil, is Russia was an ally of the United States through most of the war fighting Germany. The United States, Great Britain and other nations were fighting Germany on the Western Front and Russia was fighting Germany on the Eastern Front. The Russian people revolted against the Czar and demanded out of the war and wanted "bread for the people." This was the Bolshevik Revolution.

Fighting within the country was fierce. The Bolsheviks (Red Army) wanted out of the war. Those that disagreed with the Bolsheviks (White Army) and those that supported the Czar fought to keep the status quo. The Allies desperately wanted Russia to stay in the war to squeeze Germany from both sides. The French and British felt it necessary to send troops to Russia to support the White Army. President Wilson also agreed to help the Allies, albeit reluctantly, by sending a small contingent of American troops. They would eventually come from Camp Custer, Michigan.

The war ended, but the Americans did not come home and the fighting continued in Russia. Large battles raged while Americans continued to die. It was a political decision: France and Great Britain wanted to destroy Bolshevism, the forerunner of Communism.

At the same time, the political heat was intense from the families and media, especially from Michigan. Finally on July 4, 1919, the first contingent came home to a ticker tape parade in Detroit. Mayor James Couzens told all who attended the parade that "these men and their mission will never be forgotten." Couzens' words were formed by his lips but it was as if the world was watching a silent film. The words became vapor and most everybody forgot, for it was a time to forget wars and the ugliness that they brought.

The first part of this writing deals with the Bolshevik Revolution and why this event caused a panic in the Allied camp. The new Russian government was about to pull out of the war giving Germany a great strategic advantage. Germany would not be fighting on two fronts. The Allies began to feel that intervention in the internal affairs of Russia was necessary.

Chapter II explains the pressure that President Wilson received from the British to participate in the intervention. Wilson agreed to be involved but insisted that the American participation be minimal and our duties defensive in nature. A small American contingent from Camp Custer would be sent, along with the President's outlined American policy toward Russia in his *Aide-Memoire*.

The third theme is Detroit's reaction to this problem. While in Russia, the "Bears" were forced to endure degradation by our own Allies, causing widespread discontent on the battlefield and at home. In addition, the United States government never told them why they were in Russia and "left" them to continue fighting after the war was over. The soldiers' letters that were sent to the wives and sweethearts alarmed the families and forced them to form an organization called "Detroit's Own Welfare Association" that marched, collected recall petitions, and demanded the soldiers' return. This public anger is very common in today's world, but not so in 1919 – this was an age when the government was always right in decision making.

This was also a time when the "Red Scare" was evident in Detroit and around the country. Chapter IV deals with the widespread fear and hatred that was boiling as suspected "Red" Communists were being rounded-up and jailed; yet, our men fighting this "Red Scare" at the source, in Russia, were not honored. They had been forgotten and Michigan wanted them back!

The last chapters deal with the aftermath of the soldiers, and the political ramifications. The intervention in Russia had ended, but questions continued to be asked about the motives of the intervening powers. The Allied presence in Russia in 1919 would also color future relations between the United States and Russia.

"The men who formed the unit represented more than a dozen different nationalities... nevertheless, the one thing they did have in common, the esteem they held for the dynamic young city that they called home, was quickly expanded to embrace their new regiment; and it developed into a cohesive military organization whose loyalty and spirit were not surpassed. It carried the name 'Detroit's Own Regiment' into battle with unfailing pride and honor." – Stan Bozich, *Detroit's Own Polar Bears.*

PREFACE

After spending hundreds of hours researching and writing on this topic, I now know what fiction writers mean when they say they had no idea where the main character was headed. I thought that writing a non-fiction, straight forward historical account would destine me to a journey on a long unwinding road. But the curves came toward me fast and furious; what a ride! I unabashedly meandered into the lives of the "Polar Bear" relatives to get my story and get out – only to find myself overwhelmed by feelings of pride, sadness, and bitterness all wrapped into one. I felt pride and sadness in that they gave and suffered so much for the love of their country and bitterness, for the way that same country treated them. The curves continued as I read the letters and diaries of these men whose lives had come and gone, and ended the readings with tears of appreciation and awe. The final curve came when I talked to the two last coherent "Polar Bears": no bravado, no scorn, only humility. This is their story; the story of the "Polar Bear" and relatives alike. May my words be interpreted properly so that only honor will rest with these gallant men.

ACKNOWLEDGMENTS

My thanks to Stanley Bozich at the Military & Space Museum in Frankenmuth, Michigan for opening his priceless files to me.

FOREWORD

Roger Crownover has written a profound study of the origins of the Cold War. His book adds an essential chapter to the still unknown military and political history of the twentieth century and how the two major super-powers of the Cold War became embroiled in conflict as early as 1918 in the immediate aftermath of World War I. Even though historians and political scientists have long denied any US involvement in Russian affairs, in particular the Russian civil war and the revolutionary struggles between the Mensheviks and the Bolsheviks, Crownover sets the record straight. As he so aptly puts his case, the Great War was over but not all the boys came home. Five thousand five hundred mostly Michigan boys, "Detroit's Own," became the Polar Bears sent to fight the Bolsheviks in Northern Russian in 1919. Surely, the Great War was over but the battle for the hearts and minds of Mother Russia was heavily under way. In Crownover's words, "It was a fiasco that would haunt the United States for the next seventy years. This small but intense war between Soviet and American soldiers would be the background for what would be called the 'cold war.'"

With Russia's pullback from the War following the treaty of Brest-Litovsk in 1918 and its own civil war unfolding, both Britain and France feared the worst from a bellicose Germany fighting the west on one front alone and became suspicious of Russian and Soviet aims *vis-à-vis* Germany. Under the guise of protecting western supplies stored during the war in Russia, the Allies persuaded President Wilson to send troops to join the British and French troops in Archangel under British command to stop bolshevism and communism. Although Armistice was declared in November 1918, this incursion by the western allies and the United States lasted until summer of 1919, far, far from the western front. This book gives a thorough and insightful account of how and why the United States got involved and covered up this undeclared war.

Crownover's study is essential reading for anyone interested in US foreign affairs. He explains, with ample supporting documentation, what has become a pattern of US engagement in undeclared and even unrecorded foreign wars throughout the twentieth century. Fighting a hidden war in Northern Russia in 1919 may have been a first in the century, but the full picture must include using napalm in Greece after World War II, Korea in 1950, Iran of Mossadegh, many incursions in Central America and the Caribbean, Vietnam, the CIA-backed slayings and governmental overthrows of Patrice Lumumba in Africa, Salvador Allende in Chile and the many attempts to assassinate and overthrown Fidel Castro in Cuba. The hidden war in Cambodia in 1970 is still another significant moment in this long history.

In Michigan, home of most of the doughboys still fighting in the arctic north of Russia, the meaning of the whole adventure was carried back to the front pages and the front porches of post-war America. Sargent Matthew G. Glahek, the most decorated man in the 339th infantry battalion said,

> We had to fight to save our necks and that's what we did. We didn't know why we were fighting the Bolsheviks. We fought to stay alive.

Stanley Bozich, Michigan military historian and curator, stated,

> They were in a strange country, fighting an undeclared war under foreign officers, with unfamiliar weapons and for an uncertain cause.

They felt – and many still do – that they were rented out to the British government.

But the body bags came home nonetheless and Michigan searched for an explanation to this post-war anomaly.

The merit of Crownover's study is to complete the full story of American adventurism abroad and thus casting light on the underpinnings of the Cold War. The story of the Polar Bears is an extraordinary chapter in American history here told in a most scholarly and readable account. Learning the lessons of this untold history may yet be the only remedy to avoid future folly.

Marvin Surkin, Ph.D.
Professor of Political Science
Union Institute

CHAPTER 1

RUSSIA'S DECISION

... I have been sweating blood over the question what is right and
feasible (possible) to do in Russia. It goes to pieces like quicksilver
under my touch, ...

                      – Woodrow Wilson, July 8, 1918

"The first day I was in Camp Custer, I picked a four leaf clover. The first day
I arrived in New York at Camp Mills on our way to Russia, I picked a four leaf
clover. The first day in England, I picked a four leaf clover. After we left the boat,
I picked a four leaf clover in Russia. There was four of them that I had picked from
the time I left home until we was where the action was. I just feel I was lucky."[1]
Those were the words spoken by 95 year old Cleo Colburn in Fruitport, Michigan,
one year before he died. "I was lucky," are the words that echo through the past
seventy-seven years of time and were said by many of the other participants in this
unique event that happened at the end of World War I. The Detroit newspapers in
1919 affectionately called these men "Detroit's Own." This group officially known
as the North Russian Expeditionary Forces, or better known as the "Polar Bears,"
were 5,500 men[2] trained in Camp Custer, Battle Creek, Michigan, and sent to
Russia near the end of World War I. They immediately encountered the Bolshevik
Sixth Army of 34,700 men, led by General Boris Kuzmin. If needed, one million
Bolo's, as the Americans called the Bolsheviks, were ready in reserve.[3] All the

1

"luck" in the world was needed for anyone to survive not only the 52 degrees below zero temperature they encountered, but also the vastly larger enemy force that was thrown against them. Combined with a government that seemed to forget them, many of the "Bears" thought their luck had run out. Many, like Cleo Colburn, did survive and over the years have told a story of hardship and death that most Americans have never heard. Americans fighting and killing Russians has not been well documented in our history books. President Nixon seemed unaware of this event when, in 1972 while on a visit to Russia, he told the Russian people that we have never fought one another in war. Even President Reagan had no idea of this encounter when he made his weekly radio address to the nation, pridefully boasting, "No American boy has ever stood toe to toe against any Russian boy and as long as I am President, that will never happen."[4] George F. Kennan, the noted historian, stated that American soldiers in North Russia took "no part in any actions other than ones of a defensive nature."[5] The Polar Bear contingent would beg to differ – and so did Nikita Khrushchev in September 1959, while visiting the United States saying, "The grim days when American soldiers went to our soil headed by their generals to help our White Guard combat the new revolution. . . . Never have any of our soldiers been on American soil, but your soldiers were on Russian soil. These are the facts."[6] Even more startling is that much of the fighting and killing took place months after the armistice was signed ending World War I.

Why were American soldiers in Russia? To this day the answer is still unknown. The men were told, unofficially, that they were to defend the ammunition dumps against the Red Army (Bolsheviks). This would agree with Kennan's statement; or was their purpose to stamp out Bolshevism as Sir Winston Churchill would later state; or, another option to be considered, "Were there certain members of the cabinet of Lloyd George and of President Wilson [who] were desirous of protecting their industrial holdings in North Russia?."[7]

President Wilson specifically stated in his "Aide Memoire" (Appendix A) that United States forces would only be used to protect military stores for defensive purposes. Unbeknownst to the President, American forces were used in offensive operations against Bolshevik forces in North Russia. The American job was to defend – but things quickly changed. "On the 25th of September we unloaded the boat and on the 26th of September I was on the front line fighting. They [Bolsheviks] would hide behind trees that were cut off and take a few steps toward us. Then they would wait and take a few more steps at a time. And that's the way we fought them.

We had an engagement that very first day."[8] Their orders to be on guard duty only, did not materialize: "But we did the fighting and the British did the guarding! The British seemed to be in charge and made us do the fighting."

The first world war was a time of devastation for the entire world. Rarely in history does such a discontinuity occur that turns the world upside down overnight. But for the war, the sun might still be shining brightly over the British Isles. But for the war, there would have been no Bolshevik coup, therefore no Soviet state. But for the war, there would not have been a draconian score-settling peace that would produce a Hitler and, ultimately, the genocide of so many human beings. It was called the Great War – not in the sense of grandeur, but in the size of the horrific human devastation. It was a war that Sassoon once distilled in seven brutal lines:

'Good-morning, good-morning!' the General said
When we met him last week on our way to the line.
Now the soldiers he smiled at are most of 'em dead,
And we're cursing his staff for incompetent swine.
'He's a cheery old card,' grunted Harry to Jack

As they slogged up to Arras with rifle and pack.
But he did for them both by his plan of attack.[9]

It was a war that statesmen had threatened so freely, but which no one, in fact, had wanted – it had become inescapable. The world was "tumbling into war," as Barbara Tuchman's book, *The Guns of August* suggested, through stupidity, individual idiosyncrasies, misunderstandings, and over-zealous grandeur.

In early 1918 Russia pulled out of the war; the United States entered it. Russia abandoned its European allies; the United States came to their defense. In 1918 the Allies were able to defeat Germany and win the war, even without Russia. It was not known at the time, however, that the presence of an American army would prove more decisive than the absence of the Russians. Therefore, the United States felt pushed and shoved into a "tumbling" decision in Russia that would forever affect the lives of thousands of Americans and contribute heavily, years later, to the cold war.

There are many questions that need to be asked about the American intervention in Russia; for example, why were American troops sent to Russia in the first place? Why did they continue to fight and die after the war was over? Why were they forced to endure degradation by their own allies? And why was it necessary for the families at home to form organizations that marched, collected recall petitions, and demanded from their Congressmen the return of the soldiers? To answer these questions and more, we need an overview, albeit limited in scope, of the political and social unrest in Russia.

We begin with an overview of the conditions that existed in Russia prior to the formation of the Bolsheviks and the eventual development of the Russian Revolution. The human conditions in Russia were hard and unyielding on the common man. They had suffered for centuries under leadership that required strict obedience. When the Czar agreed to join the Allies in the fight against Germany, it was just another step in the dehumanization of the people; no voice, no choice, just obey. The war was dreadful for all, as the Russian soldier was unprepared, both militarily and physiologically – the result would be millions that would suffer and perish. The first step to break the shackles of the Czar's control began to appear in the mid-nineteenth century. This would eventually lead to the Revolution, and in its course, the marching of United States troops into Russia. This United States "interference" would leave a lasting, hostile, impression on the Russian people.

In the mid-nineteenth century the intelligentsia, who were a minority liberally educated with secular minds, grew rapidly and expressed the tradition of radicalism. This tradition was based on French and German thought.[10] Another wing, within the intelligentsia, also developed and were called the Slavophils. This group idealized the Russian past. Its precepts were to allow Russia to follow its own path of development, and not to allow Western thought to interfere with the proper, independent, development of their country.

In the nineteenth century, Russian ideas, thoughts and debates of a revolution were extremely common without interference from the government.[11] At the same time, the ruling group owned all the wealth, while enjoying immense privileges and political power, and was not about to surrender any of it to the common people. All of this brought about its inevitable accompaniment: the discontent, the frustration, and finally the explosion of the peoples' hatred toward such a system. The old system began a campaign for the suppression of free speech and censorship of books, magazines and newspapers. The people would eventually find a spark in the form of Peter Tkachev and others, who would later shape their lives drastically by instilling in them a dream – a dream of an elected parliament, a constituent assembly, in which there would be free speech and the power to frame and exercise the laws of the land.

The Czar's theme in the mid-nineteenth century was simple: Russia was not ready for democracy. To slacken the control too rapidly might cause the missions to unite and chaos would result. The Czar decided to make limited reforms, which did not appease the peasants. The dissatisfaction came from the government's strong interference in the commune (both the land and private affairs were controlled), the chronic poverty of the peasants, and the realization that even though serfdom was abolished, it was replaced by another kind of prison: economic enslavement (the redemption payments were so high the peasants were seldom able to pay the one-fifth earnest money).

Tkachev only lived to the age of forty-two and not much is known about him. Little fanfare was made of his death and burial. His life and works were not well known in his own day until men like Lenin delved deeply into his writings. Because Lenin was so enamored with Tkachev's writings, we need greater knowledge of this man. Tkachev was born on June 29, 1844, to land owning parents of modest means. He enrolled in St. Petersburg University and began studies in the law field. It was at the University that he was engulfed in a student unrest (1861), and his revolutionary ideas began to express itself. He was arrested in his first year of college for agitation against the government-appointed school administrators. It was this same year that the government decided to close the university for a time. Tkachev not only was a willing demonstrator but also showed his willingness to go to jail for his convictions. This occurred on October 12, when he and a number of other students continued to demonstrate at the University gates and were all eventually arrested and sent to the Peter and Paul Fortress. It was at this time that Tkachev listened and learned about various other revolutionaries and their programs;

"Even in the . . . Fortress. . .the students availed themselves of their free time during which they were allowed meetings. . .singing of Russian and Polish revolutionary songs, reading and writing of revolutionary poetry, and. . .endless debates on social and political topics. Many future opponents of the government became known here. . . .The sojourn in prison became for many a political school."[12] The government's determination to stop the student agitation had changed the path of his life forever. He would now spend his time as a revolutionary, writing on social and political themes.

In the year 1861, Herzen's *Bell*, among other books, was smuggled illegally into the country, proclaiming the insufficiencies of the Emancipation Decree. By the summer of 1862, the secret organization called "Land and Liberty" was formed. Its chief tenet was the belief that the primary source of all the problems destroying Russia was autocratic despotism – it was the entire political order that was wrong. Russia needed a representative assembly.

Another student outbreak occurred in 1868, and was on a larger scale than in 1861. Schools were being closed and arrests were being made as secret meetings were held between radical nonconformist students and ex-students. One of these ex-students was Peter Tkachev. One of Tkachev's key thoughts and major contributions to the Russian revolutionary ideas was the relationship between the masses and the revolutionaries. His ideas were passed on to future movements in and outside of his country. The masses needed, according to Tkachev, reeducation and psychological reconditioning. He believed that the people could not be left alone to liberate themselves. Their own efforts would only spread the old way of life. What was needed was an intellectual minority of revolutionaries providing the leadership and forming the goals for the masses. At the same time, the masses must feel that a great force had been generated in the name of their cause, uniting and enabling them to feel that force.

Lenin gave Tkachev the credit for much of his own ideology. He read all of Tkachev's literature, which appeared to leave an indelible impression upon Lenin's thinking. Lenin also used Tkachev's statistical data that the mir (village community) "had long since ceased to be virgin and had. . .[taken] the road of bourgeoisation."[13] Lenin and Tkachev felt that if the bourgeoisation in the peasantry (i.e., belief in private property, inequality of wealth) were allowed to spread, the reconstruction of a Russian society along the lines of socialism would be much harder to accomplish.

"The enamored youth receives a bitter lesson from the object of his life – to regard all persons without 'sentimentality,' to keep a stone in his sling."[14] These are the hardened words of Lenin, that not only represented the feelings of an individual, but seemingly of a nation at the end of the nineteenth century. The Czar was responsible only to God, which made the peasant feel completely helpless. But, the outrage from the people began to spring forth. Tkachev wrote an article in the first issue of *Nabat* on December 1, 1875, that said, "Do not dream, but act! Make a revolution and make it as fast as possible."[15] Others cried out for change. Men like G.V. Plekhanov, who wrote *Our Differences* in 1885, attacked the Populist movement and suggested that capitalism would be a part of this revolution (in the 1870's he was himself a Populist!). He is the acknowledged father of Russian Marxism. Plekhanov was calling for the destruction of the past, the feudal order, and the beginning of a new socialist era. "When Lenin first met him in 1895, the effect of the older man was inspirational."[16] Men like Paul Akseirod and Plekhanov were swept by the new fresh air that was penetrating Russia. They felt it mandatory to redeem the "unpaid debt" to the Russian people. They joined forces in 1879, not because they agreed in all areas (hardly the case) but through numbers they found strength. It was Plekhanov's belief that Russia's development would be similar to that of Western Europe – industrialization would have to produce a working class, before Czarism could be overthrown.[17] The Narodovoltsi, the back-to-the-peasant group, however, did not believe that Russia needed or wanted capitalism and did not need an industrial phase before the revolution could occur. A direct line from serfdom to socialism could be made. Between the years 1880 and 1882, Plekhanov began a slow change toward Marxism. His faith in the mir began to dwindle. The revolutionary "intelligentsia's only real chance was to tie its fate to that of the proletariat."[18] The proletariat could then gain the knowledge and understanding needed for the revolution.

Another notable revolutionary was Yuri Martov, a Jew in a society that oppressed Jews, dedicated his life to Marxism. His dialectical interpretation of revolutionary thought had as the synthesis the Social Democratic movement. He felt that a social revolution could not be based on any spontaneous impulse from the masses, nor from intellectuals. Only in the combining of these two forces could the revolution be successful. Unfortunately for him, Lenin never had a place for him in a leadership role. "Lenin personified the leadership of an iron vanguard; Martov was a Russian Don Quixote who expected a following not of Party troops but of an amorphous association. Lenin had proved the better leader, always with his eye on the political goal, while Martov, a naive romantic, had been sustained by the idea of injecting democratic values into the socialist program."[19]

It was the year 1887 that sent Lenin in a new direction. His brother Alexander, had gone to Petrograd to continue his studies, and there took part in the plot against Alexander III. He was caught with a bomb and condemned to death. He and the fellow conspirators were very young. He never recanted or pleaded for mercy. They were hanged on May 8, 1887. The effect upon Lenin, who had just turned seventeen, seemed to have been considerable. From this moment on, he would strike out with determination toward the revolutionary left. This enthusiasm would continue throughout his life.

In the winter of 1894, the revisionist Peter Struve met with Lenin for the first time and had a definite impression: "He hated not only the existing autocracy. . . and the bureaucracy, not only the lawlessness. . .of the police, but also their antipodes - the 'Liberals' and the 'bourgeoisie.' That hatred had something terrible and repulsive in it; for being rooted in the concrete, I should even say animal, emotions and repulsions. . . ."[20]

While Lenin was in his Siberian exile, he devised a plan to lead the Social Democracy out of a crisis, "between the forces of consciousness and the disruptive stream of diffuse 'spontaneous' impulses."[21] His plan was two fold; the first part was publishing a bimonthly journal to declare doctrine, and secondly, the beginning of a more widely distributed newspaper called the *Iskra*. *Iskra* would concentrate on the organizational and ideological areas of the movement. In this paper he stressed that in order for the successful development of the proletariat to occur, two conditions were needed: first, formulating a guide line stressing tactics that could be given to the people, and second, creating a network of organizations put together to insure the people followed in the proper "party" line.

Marxism in Russia brought together many people with conflicting ideas. Marxism had introduced an image that appealed to many. It drew those struggling for "consciousness" (those that used logic to interpret and organize life happenings), and also attracted those interested in "spontaneity" (those that used feelings and impressions to form their ideas). That was what the excitement was all about; the ability of one ideology to be acceptable to so many diverse groups of people.

The outbreak of the war in 1914 found Vladimir Llyich Ulianov, known to his revolutionary brethren and later to the world as Lenin, in exile with his wife in Zurich, Switzerland. He was broke and discontent with his life and felt, "we of the older generation may not live to see the decisive battles of this coming revolution."[22] In 1914, while the great majority of Russian peasants were clamoring for land, about 60 percent of the pig iron and 50 percent of the coal produced in Russia came from enterprises operated by French capital.[23] The Russian people were not benefiting from their own natural resources. It was a combination of these factors along with an even larger factor, World War I, that caused the crumbling of the tsarist regime. Czarist Russia was under rigid authority. The peasantry, comprising about 95 percent of the Russian population, continued to be oppressed by the authoritarian government.[24] But the people felt even more than oppression; "The problem with Russian peasants was not [just] oppression, but isolation. They were isolated from the country's political, economic, and cultural life, and therefore unaffected by the changes that had occurred since the time that Peter the Great had set Russia on the course of Westernization."[25]

A starting point for the misguided and poorly planned Allied intervention in North Russia began with the abdication of Tsar Nicholas II and the March Revolution. These events are the likely birthplace of the intervention as they represented a major change in authority and direction of Russia. The United States had not yet entered the war and Britain and France were bogged down on the Western Front. Russia was struggling with its internal quagmire and at the same time trying to stay in the war against Germany.

From the beginning of the war, it was obvious that Russian arms and equipment were totally inferior to the Germans. Russia was badly prepared for World War I. Their losses were staggering, estimated to be approximately 1.7

million dead and almost five million wounded.[26] Because of the great human loss, the government had to take raw recruits from the villages; this swelled the army with peasants who identified themselves with the people, not the official authorities. The war against Germany was not going well but the government felt safe at home. The czarist government suspected that things had reached a critical phase, but even with a war, strikes, and bread riots occurring continually, not many in the government, if any, suspected what was to take place. Lenin was at this time still in exile in Switzerland. He was thinking that at only forty-seven years of age, he was likely to die of old age before any revolution took place in Russia. He was even thinking of moving to the United States. There were few leaders of the revolution in Russia. All the future Bolshevik leaders, including Lenin and Trotsky, were living abroad, while others like Stalin and Kamenev were in prison or Siberian exile. The Bolsheviks had a skeleton staff in Russia, but its activities were restricted by the czarist police. Things seemed very safe to the government.

International Women's Day, a socialist holiday on February 23, 1917, changed the government's complacency. Not a single organization was calling for strikes because of the holiday. Even a militant Bolshevik organization was actively opposing strikes. Nevertheless, on that day, women in several textile factories went on strike. With reluctance, the other political groups felt that support must be given to the strike. It was estimated that about 90,000 workers went on strike that day.[27] The next day, the movement doubled in strength. Slogans of "Down with the Autocracy!" and "Down with the War!" became louder. Momentum was essential. The uprising had begun on February 23 with a strike; the strike had grown quickly and in three days it had become a general strike. The troops were called out and ordered to stop the marchers. Forty people were killed. As the strikers were considering an end to their disturbance because of the deaths, the special antiinsurrectionist unit , considered an elite group able to control any uprising, refused to go against the strikers. They killed their commander and sided with the people. With this mutiny happening, other units began to do the same. By nightfall, the czarist garrison was almost totally gone. The number killed, and injured was estimated at 1,315 including 587 civilians.[28] The Revolution was accomplished entirely in St. Petersburg. The czarist regime passed into history with the unconditional abdication of Nicholas II. He and his family were arrested and eventually all were murdered.[29] "The Russian Revolution of 1917 was not an event or even a process, but a sequence of disruptive and violent acts that occurred more or less concurrently but involved actors with differing and in some measure contradictory objectives. It began as a revolt of the most conservative elements in Russian society, disgusted by the Crown's . . . mismanagement of the war effort. From the conservatives the revolt spread to the liberals, who challenged the monarchy for fear that if it remained in office, revolution would become inevitable. Initially, the assault on the monarchy was undertaken not, as widely believed, from fatigue with the war but from a desire to pursue the war more effectively: not to make revolution but to avert one."[30]

The Revolution of 1917 was wonderful news for President Wilson. He ordered his Secretary of State, Robert Lansing, to cable the American Ambassador to Russia to recognize the new Provisional Government.[31] The American Ambassador to Russia, David Rowland Francis, presented himself to the new government on March 22, 1917, thus becoming the first country to offer official recognition.[32]

The revolution played an important part in President Wilson's decision to enter the war as was clearly indicated in his message to Congress recommending the declaration of war on Germany:

Does not every American feel that assurance has been added to our hope for the future peace of the world by the wonderful and heartening things that have been happening within the last few weeks in Russia? Russia was known by those who knew it best to have been always in fact democratic at heart, in all the vital habits of her thought, in all the intimate relationships of her people that spoke their natural instinct, their habitual attitude towards life. The autocracy that crowned the summit of her political structure, long as it had stood and terrible was the reality of its power, was not in fact Russian in its origin, character, or purpose; and now it has been shaken off and the great, generous Russian people have been added in all their naive majesty and might to the forces that we are fighting for freedom in the world, for justice , and for peace. Here is a fit partner for a league of honor.[33]

The United States declared war on Germany on April 16,1917. The United States Army probably would never have entered Russia if the Russian Revolution had proceeded as first planned. After the tsarist government was eliminated, there developed a power vacuum. The Provisional Government took office on the abdication of the Tsar. It was composed of ten Liberals and one Socialist who endeavored to do the impossible; encompass loyalty to the Allies and placate Russia's war-weariness. It failed miserably due to the following three factors: first, it lacked enforcement of its authority; second, it lacked the support of tradition that the monarchy enjoyed; and third, it failed to generate any new support on its own. Some of the leaders were Prince Gregori Lvov, Paul Miliukov, Alexander Guchkoff, Michael Tereschenko, and Alexander Kerensky. Miliukov would later write: "To make you understand [the] special character of the Russian Revolution, I must draw your attention to [the] peculiar features, made our own by the whole process of Russia's history. To my mind, all these features converge into one. The fundamental difference which, distinguishes Russia's social structure from that of other civilized countries, can be characterized as a certain weakness or lack of a strong cohesion or cementation of elements which form a social compound. You can observe that lack of consolidation in the Russian social aggregate in every aspect of civilized life: political, social, mental and national."[34]

The Provisional Government's initial foreign policy seemed to show it had failed to grasp the gravity of the situation. The Russian people wanted out of the war immediately. The ending of the war was the catalyst in removing the tsarist regime. The people had called for "Peace, Bread, Land" and the new government was giving them more war! The Provisional Government was to be in charge until a constituent assembly could be elected by the people. Its revolutionary program would include: amnesty for political prisoners, freedom of speech, equal rights for all citizens, and the defense of the country against the enemy in the west. The first order of business was to restore order and honor to Russia. The "honor" would include a victory in the fight against the Germans. The Allied Governments found this statement most gratifying as it would insure the continuation of Russia in the war against Germany.

At the same time, there was in session in Petrograd, the Soviet of Workers', Soldiers', and Peasants' Deputies. It had been elected on March 10, before the end of the Czar's regime. The men and women who physically fought for the Revolution considered the Petrograd Soviet as the only body of authority. This body was controlled by Prince Tseretelli and the Menshevik Party. The Bolshevik party was a very small part of the Soviet at this time. It is widely agreed that the Soviet represented the feelings of the masses more than did the Provisional Government. It also controlled many of the troops, railroads, postal and telegraph services. The Soviet acted as the official body of government in declaring to the world the desire of the Russian worker to end the war. The world was hearing two voices from Russia, both claiming authority.

In Switzerland, Lenin was surprised by the Revolution. In the three weeks that followed the upheaval (March 20 - April 8), Lenin stayed in close contact with what was happening and wrote five letters to the Bolshevik faction for their edification and guidance. The letters touched upon the problems of the Revolution and the course needed by the revolt to attain the ultimate goal – dictatorship of the proletariat.

He was correct in assessing the inability of the Provisional Government to satisfy the desire of the Russian people; the desire was an end to the war.

The Petrograd Soviet and the Provisional Government were to govern revolutionary Russia for the next eight months. There were many problems and contradictions that would eventually help the Bolsheviks gain control. The dual system of government had the Provisional Government on one side representing the propertied classes, Mensheviks, the Bolsheviks and the SR's (Social-Revolutionaries), while the Soviet of Workers' Deputies represented the soldiers. It was agreed upon by both groups that the revolution would be for political and religious freedoms, freedom of speech, press, assembly, and strikes and freedom for trade unions. At the beginning of the revolution, it was meant to be a government somewhat patterned after the ideals of the United States.

The new government had no power: no dependable armed forces, no trained bureaucracy, and very little support from the armed masses whose sole concern was stopping the war. Within this twin power-head came two opposing sides. The extreme right wing was the Kadets, the party representing what had been known as the liberal bourgeoisie before the revolution and now was the "bastion of conservatism." They wanted a republic with a Western like constitution and a continuation of war against Germany. The Bolshevik party was at the other extreme and their entire campaign was directed at ending the war. It was not until Lenin appeared that the party became an effective fighting force. In fact, his appearance on April 3, 1917, changed the entire development of the revolution. No other socialist group had even thought of doing what he had in mind – maneuver for power! He would be the first to think of a one man power controlling the revolution and the country. What this meant was clear; future victories were not for the Revolution but for the Bolsheviks. They seemed to be the only group that was saying what the masses wanted to hear: Peace, Bread, Land! "The attitude of the Bolsheviks was absolutely clear; down with the war and an immediate peace at all costs."

Russia's war effort had been steadily declining, and the Allies now hoped for a renewed effort. The United States immediately began negotiations to establish more credit for Russia, however, the internal matters in Russia were beginning to boil. Milyukov, on May 1, in his capacity as Foreign Minister, advised the Allies that Russia would fight to the end and his country would live up to the agreed upon summer offensive. In other words, all treaties and obligations were still valid. On May 3, crowds in the streets demonstrated against this decision. The next day shooting broke out.

Trotsky arrived in Russia on May 17 and officially became a Bolshevik in July, the same month that the Russian offensive began against the Germans. Both Lenin and Trotsky were bitterly against the continued fighting. The last major offensive began July 1, and the troops, even though battle-worn, fought fiercely in the beginning. On July 19, the Germans counter-attacked. Morale was so low by this date that regiment after regiment revolted, murdered their officers, and retreated. Bolshevik sympathizers had successfully penetrated each unit and the rout was on.

In the papers of the Czar and Alexandra, made public years later, was found a poem in Alexandra's hand. It was written by S.S. Bekhteev, a brother of Zinaida Tolstoy, a close friend of the royal family. It represented the inner feelings of the royal family but it also manifested the soul of a nation crying out for spiritual help in its time of need.

> Give patience, Lord, to us Thy children
> In these dark, stormy days to bear
> The persecution of our people,
> The tortures falling to our share.
> Give strength, Just God, to us who need it
> The persecutors to forgive,
> Our heavy, painful cross to carry
> And Thy great meekness to achieve.
> When we are plundered and insulted,
> In days of mutinous unrest,
> We turn for help to Thee, Christ-Savior,
> That we may stand the bitter test.
> Lord of the world, God of Creation
> Give us Thy blessing through our prayer,
> Give peace of heart to us, O Master,
> This hour of deadly dread to bear.
> And on the threshold of the grave
> Breathe power divine into our clay
> That we, Thy children, may find strength
> In meekness for our foes to pray.[35]

Back in Petrograd, two more days of street fighting took place, but finally the Provisional Government gained the upper hand. The Bolsheviks were not prepared to take advantage of the situation. Kerensky, relieved for the moment that the Bolsheviks had failed, turned his attention to the reorganization of the Government. On July 22 he formed a Cabinet that included all parties except the Monarchists and the Bolsheviks. General Kornilov was appointed head of the armies and was ordered to stop the German advance. Kerensky issued another letter to the Allies assuring them of their continual fight. Unfortunately for Kerensky, the fighting was a total disaster for the Russian Army. The capture of Riga by the Germans on September 3 brought Petrograd within striking distance – the front had disintegrated.

Even General Kornilov turned against Kerensky and attempted a military *coup d'etat* during the second week of September. It failed as Kerensky armed the populace to help repel Kornilov. The decision to arm the people would eventually lead to his own demise.

In November, after many skirmishes and an armed populace against him, Kerensky's regime ended.

Kerensky escaped and would never return. Lenin and his cohorts seized power in Petrograd and seemingly caught the Allied diplomatic corps in Petrograd off guard. The Bolshevik program demanded an immediate peace with the Central Powers. Rumors were increasing among the Allies that the Bolshevik leaders, Lenin and Trotsky, were German agents who had returned to Russia with the assistance of Germany.[36] The Allies hoped for the "sane" elements in Russia to eventually win out. At the same time the British and French governments were aiding counterrevolutionary movements in south and southeast Russia. To the Allies, keeping Russia in the war became a major concern. The Russian army was needed to keep a "two front" war against Germany. Could the Bolsheviks be persuaded to keep Russia in the fight, or would they

seek a separate peace with Germany, thereby ending the fighting at the Eastern front? Unfortunately for the Allies, Lenin was not a man seemingly able to digest anything other than the Revolution at hand; ". . . Lenin thought about nothing but revolution, day and night, and even dreamt about it; such a man was impossible to have dealings with."[37]

On December 29, 1917, the first official diplomatic request to the United States concerning intervention came from Great Britain. The American Ambassador to Great Britain, Walter Hines Page,[38] cabled to Lansing that the British were considering a policy that called for the protection of Allied military stores in Russia.

A few days later, on January 8, 1918, Wilson gave his "Fourteen Points" speech to Congress. Point VI was directed toward Russia. Wilson called for the "evacuation of all Russian territory" and a "settlement that would allow for self determination." Wilson felt the Bolshevik regime did not represent the true feelings of the Russian people. The "Self determination" clause expressed Wilson's idea that the Bolsheviks did not constitute a democratic institution that could govern Russia. The regime had seized power during a time of great turmoil, and therefore, Wilson rationalized, should not be considered legitimate.[39] This distrust between the Bolsheviks and United States governments would linger for over seventy years. "Even when Herbert Hoover, head of the U.S. Food Administration, launched a relief program in July 1921 to help distribute food and combat the famine in Russia, most of the workers being young American students, Lenin sensed danger. He wrote secretly to Molotov: 'In view of the agreement with the American, Hoover, there is going to be an influx of a mass of Americans. We should think about surveillance and being kept informed.'"[40]

Wilson's decision to intervene in Russia, however reluctantly, was based on several reasons. Besides a distrust for the new Bolshevik government, winning the war was the first and most important goal; if Russia fell to the Germans, it could cause a disaster. The Allies also stressed the need for an American involvement to show the world that the Allies were in agreement.

The French and British were panicstricken when Russia withdrew from the war by the treaty of Brest-Litovsk on March 3, 1918. The terms stripped Russia of one-third of her territory, including the Ukraine, Finland, Poland, and the Baltic lands.[41] Many Russians were especially outraged that the agreement gave away one-third of Russia's crop land, half of her industrial capacity, and sixty-two million people who were no longer part of the empire. However, other parts of the treaty were more to the liking of the people, for example, the Russian soldiers on the Eastern Front were told to stop fighting. It was thought that only through peace could the Bolshevik regime survive.[42]

The Soviet also declared that all treaties of the former Russian government were now invalid.[43] The Germans were ecstatic, as this would allow thousands of Germans to be free for duty on the Western Front. The Allies were in panic, believing that they could not withstand the "steamroller" effect of the Germans heading toward the English Channel. Terror had griped France and Great Britain as intervention seemed inevitable. The President resisted, but realized force was becoming necessary in Russia. The Allies, along with Wilson, believed Lenin had betrayed their cause against Germany. The Allies concentrated all their attention on the evils of Germany. "There was a tendency to exaggerate German ambitions and the German role in Russia; to underestimate the disunity in the Germany camp and the weaknesses and limitations that rested on the German war effort; to underrate the phenomenon of Bolshevism as an indigenous manifestation of Russian political realities; to regard the confusions of the Russian scene as only another projection of German evil; and to argue from this that the problems of Russia, like those of Europe proper, would find their solution automatically in an Allied victory over Germany."[44]

There was a major concern about the stockpiles of supplies stored in Northern Russia. Would the enemy get to them? Would the Bolsheviks simply give the Germans the supplies? These questions were foremost in the minds of many. "The British fears were reasonable enough. The Germans intended to do just what the British general staff suspected: to make a deal with the Russians to take over those military supplies and turn them back against the Allies. A German military mission was in Moscow when the occupation of the port of Archangel began."[45] The Allies decided their only hope for victory in the war was to stop the revolution ; intervention was necessary.

Winston Churchill called the intervention necessary to "strangle Bolshevism at birth." President Wilson added additional reasons for intervention so as to prevent military stores from falling into the hands of the Germans and to foster Russian self-determination. Reports arriving on Wilson's desk seemed to show the Russian people were not behind the Bolsheviks. "A mission headed by Elihu Root reported after a visit that German propaganda was undermining the Russians' will to fight so that the Army was falling to pieces and the 'socialistic element' was increasing its influence. Most of the old divisions of the empire were seeking to breakaway from it [the Bolsheviks], while even in Petrograd and Moscow the Bolsheviks had to ally themselves with terrorists in order to maintain their power."[46] Wilson "hated to do this [intervention], and agreed only because he had refused so many other Allied requests."[47] It would be hard for Wilson to admit this mistake later when the war had ended. Furthermore, how to bring the troops home without fanfare would be his perplexing question.

Ambassador Francis was convinced that Lenin and Trotsky were paid German Agents. He would later write in his memoir that "Lenin was first sent as a German agent to demoralize the Russian Army and withdraw Russia from the war. His administration has been marked with murder and theft."[48] The ambassador claimed that Lenin was working for Germany, who could "benefit greatly from Russia's resources and military stores."[49] The fear of Allied supplies falling in the hands of the Germans was real, but it was minute compared to the prospect of German troops leaving the Eastern Front and concentrating on the West. It was also alarming to the Allies that Germany might recruit Russians into her armies. General John J. Pershing was concerned that German recruiting from the Russian peasant class, could make a Russian army into a very potent fighting force in a very short time.[50] By the time Allied forces arrived in Russia, the Bolsheviks had already seized all the Western war supplies in the Siberian Area. The situation in Russia was in chaos. Yet Wilson still intervened, even against the advice of many of his military planners. "A serious military mistake," was said by the Army Chief of Staff General Peyton C. March and General Pershing was also completely against it.[51] The stage was now set for making the crucial decision to intervene in Russia.

At the request of the British Government, President Wilson acquiesced and dubiously consented to send the 339th Infantry Regiment, 1st Battalion of the 310th Engineers, the 337th Field Hospital, and the 337th Ambulance Company, all of which were detached from the 85th "Custer" Division. The Americans constituted about one-third of the total Allied contingent of 15,000 men. Approximately eighty-five percent of the 5500 Americans were from Michigan, and seventy percent of those men were from Detroit.[52]

This constituted a very small force sent to combat the entire Bolshevik army.

Even this concession of President Wilson was limited to the one regiment of infantry with the needed accompaniments of engineer and medical troops. The bitter irony of this limitation is apparent in the fact that while it allowed the Supreme War Council to carry out its scheme of an Allied Expedition with the publicly announced purposes before outlined, committing America and the other Allies to the guarding of supplies at Murmansk and Archangel and frustrating the plans of Germany in North Russia, it did not permit the Allied War Council sufficient forces to carry out its ultimate and of course secret purpose of reorganizing the Eastern Front, which naturally was not to be advertised in advance either to Russians or to anyone. The vital aim was thus thwarted and the expedition destined to weakness and to future political and diplomatic troubles both in North Russia and in Europe and America.[53]

The United States soldiers were on their way, unknowingly, to be the first (and only) American soldiers to fight on Russian soil. Unfortunately for them, the world was not paying attention: "The outside world heard muffled reverberations of the Bolshevik terror from newspaper accounts, reports of visitors, and Russian refugees. Some reacted with revulsion, a few with sympathy: but the prevalent response was one of indifference."[54]

CHAPTER II

THE POLAR BEARS AND
THE SACRIFICIAL COMMITMENT

It is the matter of the most complex and difficult sort, and I have at
no time felt confident in my own judgment about it.

– Woodrow Wilson

No word comes, and the soldier is left to think that he has been
abandoned by his own country, left to rot. . . !

– Lt. Cudahy

The first contingent of enlisted men arrived at Camp Custer, Michigan, during

the week of September 6, 1917. They were greeted by Colonel John W. Craig, the

commanding officer of the 339th Infantry Regiment. They became part of the 85th

Division, which consisted of the 337th, 338th, 339th, and 340th Infantry. The 337th

was the unit picked for Russian service. Since most of the men of the 337th, officers

and enlisted, were from Detroit, the nickname "Detroit's Own Regiment" soon took

hold. The recruits came from all walks of life – farms and factories alike; with many

different nationalities, and in some cases, lacking in the English language. Being

midwesterners would help them to be somewhat physically attuned to the cold

weather that would be in their future. They all had high esteem for the city that they

called home (Detroit) and, "it developed into a cohesive military organization whose

loyalty and spirit were not surpassed. It carried the 'Detroit's Own Regiment' into

battle with unfailing pride and honor."[55] There would eventually be 20,000 officers

and enlisted men ready for training in the 85th Division. Also training at Camp

25

Custer was the 310th Engineers, the 337th Field Hospital and 337th Ambulance Companies. (Three Companies of the 310th would also go to Russia along with 225 men from the 337th Hospital and ambulance).

In Washington, the question as to what to do about Russia was still unanswered. The idea of intervening militarily into this vast land gave the Allies cause for hesitation. Should the United states, along with other Allied countries, intervene directly into the internal affairs of another sovereign country? Such a decision could result in either a thoroughly disastrous maneuver, or a brilliant victorious march into history.[56] If the decision was made to enter, how could it be justified to the world? President Wilson pondered this problem at great length. Would the world perceive it as an invasion of a neutral country? Eventually, Wilson came to feel that the decision to intervene should be presented solely in the context of the war against the Kaiser; the ramifications were not considered until after the war. The answer came quickly from an unexpected source, Trotsky himself. Trotsky received a telegram from an official at the Brest-Litovsk Treaty signing, stating that there was a concern for the Russian delegation's safety. It was uncertain if the Germans would keep their word. Trotsky misinterpreted it to mean that the Germans were advancing and the delegation needed protection. Trotsky had already received a cable from the Allies offering aid if Germany became aggressive. To deal with the immediate crisis, Trotsky cabled the delegation to accept Allied assistance, if necessary. It was meant only for this situation, but the Allies used it as a basis for future intervention.[57]

On March 21, 1918, the Brest-Litovsk Treaty was signed. Immediately, the Germans, as expected by the Allies, moved many of the eastern divisions to the western front. The Allies were in trouble as the full force of the German army was now directed westward; the request to send troops to Russia became louder. But how many troops could be spared from the French line? The answer became painfully evident; there were very few available. Wilson, however, continued to resist intervention.

Despite the Brest-Litovsk peace agreement, the Allies felt that Germany was still a threat to Russia. In January of 1918, the suggestion was made to Ambassador Francis to move the embassy from Petrograd to Sweden. Francis, although understanding the safety of this move, was against it. He felt that if the Allies left Russia, the Germans would take advantage of this decision to occupy the country. He eventually relented but only moved to Vologda. This provided an easier escape route in case the Germans or the Red Army came too close. The town was situated near the Moscow-Archangel railway and the Trans-Siberian railway intersect, which would allow an escape in several directions. It would also serve as a strategic outpost should the Allies decide to intervene.

The Germans had issued an ultimatum to the Bolshevik government stating that, if the Allies did not leave Russia, it would be a violation of the treaty and "consequences will be grave and Germany will take action in Russia."[58]Francis was against any evacuation as he believed that most Russians wanted an Ally intervention. The Ambassador's feelings were conveyed to President Wilson.

Back at Camp Custer, many of the men were hurriedly trained and sent off to divisions already overseas. Some of the officers at the camp, were doing all they could to hold on to their ablest men. "As the men poured into Camp Custer we would get orders from headquarters to send . . . men . . . fully equipped and ready for overseas duty. Of course the orders always read to send the best-qualified and trained men. . . . On consulting with the other shavetails of the regiment, I found that we all did the same thing. Instead of sending the best-qualified men we kept those men longest in the company and sent the newest recruits (to fight). Sometimes the poor lads hadn't even been taught squads left and squads right yet. . . ."[59] To fill the ranks, new recruits continued to arrive. Some were given three or four months of good training. Others were not so lucky as, Cleo Colburn recalled, "We had a total of three weeks training. . . . That was all!"[60] Finally, "Someone somewhere decided that we had idled away enough time in Camp Custer and were now prepared physically and mentally to save the world for democracy. Orders were given out to be ready to pack up and to go through numerous inspections so that nothing would be left out, and to be ready to leave Camp Custer in July, 1918."[61] July came and the 85th Division was ordered overseas. They boarded trains for the New York area and arrived at Camp Mills, Long Island, the next day. One week later they departed for England. Everybody expected the next stop to be France where their fighting would begin. On arriving in England, the unexpected happened. The 339th Infantry Regiment, along with the First Battalion of the 310th Engineers, the 337th Ambulance Company, and the 337th Hospital Company separated, and the rest of the Division (337th, 338th, and 340th) left for France. Excitement abounded amongst the remaining men. Would they be stationed in England? Was there an angelic host watching over them? This delirious bubble would soon burst. Lieutenant Harry Mead, as part of the 339th Infantry, was enjoying his stay until he met an old friend. The story is told by Lieutenant Mead's son, Hudson Mead: "I'll tell you, that is a pretty good story . . . . My father went to school in Indiana, and his mother, to make ends, took in college students, and one of the students came from a little town in Colorado and his name was Lowell Thomas. And so they became fast friends and at that time led different careers. So now we move up to World War I and they [troops] landed in England. Pa got a pass to see London. Who does he run into, but Lowell Thomas. . . . Thomas can't wait to tell a secret and says, 'Guess where you guys are going?' 'France, to win the war? [was the reply].' Thomas says, 'Don't be silly, Harry, you're going to North Russia. . . . When you get back to camp take notice.' My father then said he began to notice that heavy clothing was coming in boxes. He would later recall, 'Come to think of it, there were some skis and things'. I believe that was the first word given to any of the men."[62]

Wilson agreed with the Allies that the war supplies that had been previously shipped by the Allies to the former Russian government, must be protected. "These included valuable stocks of metals: 2,000 tons of aluminum, 2,100 tons of antimony, 14,000 tons of copper, 5,230 tons of lead, etc. . . . Not only had these supplies been provided by the Allies from their own scarce wartime stocks, but they had been in effect paid for as well by the Allies under the credits extended to Russian governments, and had been shipped in the extremely scarce Allied tonnage, desperately needed in other theaters of war."[63] One estimate had the value at one billion dollars:"On the docks and in the warehouses were piled a billion dollars' worth of war material shipped largely from the United States and Japan for the Russian war effort against Germany."[64]

The English believed that to avoid a German steamroller heading toward the English Channel, the Revolution must be stopped. It was also Sir Winston Churchill's intentions to strangle Bolshevism at its birth. Japan's territorial aspirations were another factor. Documents reveal that once Japan had indicated her intentions to undertake an independent expedition to Siberia and Northern Manchuria, the United States felt they had to act.[65] It was suggested by the Allies that Japan be allowed to enter Russia as a military force to help the so called White Army fight the Red Army. President Wilson was strongly opposed to the suggested Japanese expedition. He felt that the Japanese themselves had originated the plan for invading Russia and that they wanted it to be exclusively Japanese. The mere fact that Japan had now become an ally was not sufficient to put aside Wilson's suspicions of her. Wilson felt that

Japan would easily drop the British for a German alliance if Germany offered a better deal. "American distrust of Japan was clearly revealed in Wilson and Arthur J. Balfour, British Foreign Minister, regarding a proposed naval agreement, which was to be directed against Japanese as well as against German aggression."[66] The United States did not want Japan in Russia. (The Japanese did eventually enter Siberia but not Northern Russia). It was reported that a strong anti-American campaign by the Japanese at home and in Russia was under way. The Japanese were trying to persuade the Russians to place the entire intervention in their hands. Some of their reports even suggested that the Americans had agreed with Germany to divide and share Russia.[67]

At home, too, Wilson was bombarded by interventionist. Ambassador Francis and many in the State Department were anti-Bolshevik and wanted intervention. For Wilson, the decision to intervene was extremely difficult. He had reluctantly entered the war and now he faced the possibility of massive bloodshed in a land that most of his advisors knew nothing about. However, the ruined Romanov empire lay "writhing in agony like a snake run over on the road."[68]

On June 1, 1918, the decision by Wilson was made to intervene with a limited number of troops. The news made headlines in the United States. Many papers carried similar headlines such as, "U.S. Now To Act In Russia; Sammies Win New Praise," and, "Allies Are Anxious".[69] The American public was given the situation:

Heretofore the hope of the American government has been that Russia might be helped solely by peaceful means. It is realized, however, that all these plans will require time to execute and that in the meantime Germany is busy extending and tightening her grasp upon the disorganized country and actually building a grave menace to the allies in the far east. The allied spokesmen have reported that instead of improving, internal conditions of Russia are going from bad to worse. The Bolshevik government has conceded German demands aimed at the political integrity of the country and is declared to have shown no disposition to conciliate the elements in opposition, embodying the best of the Russian people.[70]

"President Wilson – acting reluctantly, against his own better judgment and that of his military advisors, and only with a view to conciliating the European Allies – agreed to yield to [their] judgment."[71] Not all of Wilson's advisors were for the intervention. Many in the military were not. "A serious military mistake," was said by the Army Chief of Staff General Peyton C. March. General John J. Pershing stated in his memoirs, "When our Ambassador to Russia, Mr. David R. Francis, was in Paris. . . he strongly advocated our intervention and thought 100,000 men would save the nation. He urged me to recommend it, but I was opposed . . . . The fact is that the tendency persisted . . . to send expeditions here and there in pursuit of political aims. They were prone to lose sight of the fundamental fact that the real objective was the German Army."[72]

The decision to intervene was made at a meeting attended by Secretary of State Lansing, Secretary of War Baker, Secretary of the Navy Josephus Daniels, Chief of Staff General Peyton C. March, Chief of Naval Operations Admiral William S. Benson, and the President. Wilson outlined the policy of the United States toward Russia in his "Aide Memoire" (Appendix A) that approved the participation of the United States in the Allied intervention. This document is essential to note in determining the official stance of the American soldier in Russia compared to what actually occurred. It began by stating that the United States would support other Allied Governments in defeating the enemy but it would only take action other than in France. Diplomats would later ignore the following part of the document:

" It (American Government) wishes to cooperate in every practicable way with the Allied Governments, and to cooperate ungrudgingly; for it has no end of its own to serve and believes that the war can be won only by common counsel and . . . action. . . .Military intervention there would add to the present sad confusion in Russia rather than cure it, injure her rather than help her, and that it would be of no advantage in the prosecution of our main design, to win the war against Germany. . . .Military action is inadmissible in Russia. . . . The only legitimate object for which American or Allied troops can be employed, it submits, is to guard military stores which may subsequently be needed by Russian forces and to render such aid as may be acceptable to the Russians in the organization of their own self-defense. . . .

None of the governments uniting in action. . . contemplates any interference of any kind with the political sovereignty of Russia, any intervention in her internal affairs, or any impairment of her territorial integrity either now or hereafter. . . . It feels that it ought to add, also, that is will feel at liberty . . . to withdraw these forces. . . if the plans in whose execution it is now intended that they should cooperate should develop into others inconsistent with the policy to which the Government of the United States feels constrained to restrict itself.[73] "

It was plainly stated by Wilson, that the United States would not be involved in any military intervention. Only a limited, guarding action, would be accepted by the American force. The entire document was one of self determination by the Russian people, whether it be by the Bolsheviks or some other force. Wilson showed reluctance to send Americans to Russia and was clear in his right to pull the troops out if they were misused. The "limiting action" and "misuse" of the troops would be ignored by several diplomats involved in the operation, most notably Francis, and the British command. Both parties had an additional idea in mind; the elimination of the Russian Bolshevik government! The Polar Bears would be the pawns that Francis would so discreetly maneuver.

General John J. Pershing was directed by the War Department to dispatch troops to North Russia to join the Allied expedition. Lenin, in his speech to the Soviet Central Committee on July 29, considered it an invasion: "[The] imperialists will do their very utmost to overthrow the Soviet Government. . . . We face a systematic. . . long-planned . . . campaign against the Soviet Republic. . . . We are now at war with British and French [and soon American] imperialism."[74]

The Wilson American plan began to change immediately, even before arriving in Russia. By agreement between the American and British commands, the American units were placed under the British command, in the transportation and supply units. They were immediately stripped of GI gear and given the long and clumsy Russian Mosin-Nagant bolt-action rifles. New England Westinghouse and Remington had been making these weapons and supplying them to Russia since 1914.[75] The Americans disliked them as soon as they were put into their hands.

The GI's were fond of their Enfields, and now they were given these "ugly rifles" with bayonets attached to them without scabbards; with the sights calibrated in Russian paces instead of yards. Of course, as soon as these weapons were issued, the men had an idea of their destination. Confirmation came when they were also issued socks, sweaters, and undershirts; all made of wool. The date of issue for these items was August, 1918 in England. The days and nights were hot, and it did not take long for the GI's to put two and two together. They were also supplied with British Vickers, water-cooled machine guns chambered for Russian ammunition. Unfortunately, "Such armaments were guaranteed to freeze in arctic temperatures."[76] The winter gear given to the Americans by the British proved about as good as the weapons. They were given Shackleton Boots (named for a British antarctic explorer), but the Americans often wore Russian Valilnkas, a knee-high boot lined with fur material. The Shackleton boots were warm and comfortable, but they were impractical for any one who had to move about or march through deep snow. The soles were made of very stiff but smooth leather, which offered no traction on the slippery snow and ice. An example of what could and did happen because of the High Command's mistake, took place when Company A was forced to make a retreat from Shenkursk. Many of the men found it impossible to continue the march in these boots. They threw them away to save their lives and kept going in their bare feet, suffering severe frostbite.[77] Many of the new recruits had a total of three weeks in training at Fort Custer and now they were issued all new articles of clothing, rifles, machine guns, bayonets, and grenades. They practiced day and night to become accustomed to the weapons. They had perfected the handling of the Colt and the Browning, and were ready as much as possible in that short of time, to fight on equal terms with the enemy. "The American Doughboy in the North Russian campaign mastered every kind of weapon that was placed in his hands or came to him by fortune of war. He learned to use the Lewis and Vickers machine guns, also the One Pounder, or Pom-Pom. He had to adapt or die. He was given warm but impractical clothing, quick training, and made to serve under a foreign command; and then be thrown into an enemy that outnumbered them sixty to one!"[78]

"Soldiers of the United States, the people of the British Isles welcome you on your way to take your stand. . . for human freedom. . . ." These hand written words were given to each GI on board ship as they got closer and closer to Russia. The small letter, written and signed in long hand by King George the 5th, was very impressive. It was impressive because it was made to look as if each GI received an original. Instead, they were very well done copies.[79] The sailing proved ill-fated for some. After leaving from England,   Spanish influenza struck the 339th. Seventy-nine men died.

As the Americans clambered down the gangplank and touched Russian soil with their feet, they may have touched the dirt, just to see if the earth felt the same as home. Most of these boys had not traveled more than 50 miles from their Michigan farms in their entire lives. To their dismay, it was the only thing that seemed the same. The area was 330,000 square miles of tundra, swamps with thick fir forests, and snow, ice, and rain all falling together. It was the gloomiest, most inhospitable place any of these men had ever seen. To lose a mitten was to risk losing a hand. "Left Camp Custer July 11, 1918 – 14 day crossing to England. . . . Left England Aug. 26 for Russia. Arrived Sept. 4. Slept in a swamp all night and it was raining so we had no place to lay so we did not do any sleeping but walked back and forth all night to keep from freezing."[80] The men knew what cold weather was like, being from the Midwest, but they never thought it could ever get that cold. "It was 52 below zero when we arrived. We had to change guards every fifteen minutes because it was so cold."[81](see footnote) Very few of the men were lucky enough to be billeted with a Russian family in a typical log house. Those that did, describe the homes as unattractive but warm, with a giant stove in the middle of the small home. Some members of the families, usually the parents or grandparents, would sleep on the top of the huge stoves. It was also very common for the Russians to keep their livestock indoors in a separate back room. The men had a hard time getting use to the smell and also to the thousands of cockroaches swarming in every direction.[82] The Russians and the

Amerikanski guest got along   very well. Well enough, in fact, that eight Americans took Russian wives home with them. The question was asked of one of the Americans as to why the Russians accepted them so easily. His answer was, "If somebody armed with a rifle decided to invite himself into your house, I guess you'd be rather hospitable yourself."[83] Most of the men, however, slept in wood piles. Most never even knew of any one who slept in a home. "Our dugouts was [sic] wood piles. They fired their engines with wood and lots of it around. We'd stick our rifles in the ground with the bayonets and that's where we would sleep."[84]

Ambassador Francis was following his own agenda. He was firmly anti-Bolshevik and now that the United States had made its commitment, he would use the troops to rid the world of this menace. To his defense (admittedly weak), he may have misinterpreted the *Aide-Memoire*. After first reading it, he wired the State Department, "that although it was 'mystifying on first reading,' it appeared 'admirably adapted to Russian situation. . . . I shall endeavor to follow policy outlined when American troops arrive.'"[85] He would later write, "I shall. . . encourage American troops. . . to proceed to such points in the interior as Kotlas, Sukhona, and Vologda, as at those places, as well as in Petrograd and Moscow, are stored war supplies which the Soviet government, in violation of its promises and agreements, transferred from Archangel." In other words, Francis took the message from the President to mean any military advancement and engagement was acceptable, even in invading Moscow itself, to regain the supplies. Francis had a great admiration and devotion to the President but it was obvious his intentions were opposite to those of Wilson's. E.M. Halliday states that, "There is thus a wryly comic aspect to the conversation, reported by Francis in his memoirs, which occurred when Steward [Colonel George E. Stewart, commander of the U.S. Expeditionary Force in North Russia] came to see the ambassador shortly after the arrival of the 339th Infantry. After pointing out that he was the official interpreter of United States policy in Russia, Francis said, 'If I should tell you not to obey one of General Poole's[86] orders what would you do?' Stewart answered, 'I would obey you.' . . . If. . . he had been thinking of the glaring contradiction between Poole's military actions against the Bolsheviks and President Wilson's insistence on peaceful intervention, the whole shape of Allied action at Archangel might have been different – possibly with far-reaching results in terms of later relations between the government of the Soviet Union and that of the United States. . . .Apparently it never convincingly occurred to Francis that in permitting the use of American troops for an offensive action deep into the Russian interior he was violating the United States policy. . . ."[87]

Francis decided that "to guard military stores" meant the United States Army could leave their assigned duties, travel hundreds of miles into Russia to engage themselves against the Bolsheviks.

At the same time, Francis was receiving encouragement from the State Department. Contradictory statements were being sent by the State Department as if no one was bothering to read Francis' reports: "Department approves your action fully. Determine your future course by careful compliance with policy communicated to you"[88] The policy communicated to Francis was the *Aide-Memoire.* Francis had stretched his authority completely out of proportion, but his government continued to applaud his actions.

On September 26, another letter, even more specific, was sent by Secretary Lansing to Francis. At the time of this letter, General Poole was engaged in an offensive operation that was composed largely of members of the 339th Infantry. The letter read: ". . .we shall insist with the other governments, so far as our cooperation is concerned, that all military effort in northern Russia be given up except guarding of the ports. . . ."[89] Francis paid no attention to this report as his plan was continuing to unfold. His attitude was similar to a quote by Napoleon: "You commit yourself and then – you see."

Meanwhile, in Washington, Wilson was worried over his decision. He wrote his friend, Victor F. Lawson, "It is the matter of the most complex and difficult sort, and I have at no time felt confident in my own judgment about it."[90] It was obvious it was an agonizing decision, as other letters he wrote had a similar sound. To Professor Masaryk, another good friend, he writes, "I have felt no confidence in my personal judgment about the complicated situation in Russia, and am reassured that you should approve what I have done."[91]

On September 4, American troops landed at Archangel under the command of Colonel George Stewart, a Medal of Honor recipient for his part in the Spanish-American War. However, the medal was not gathered through a military operation. It was during the Philippine insurrection on the island of Panay, November 26, 1899, when he saved an Englishman from drowning.

Archangel was at one time a very cosmopolitan city. Englishman Richard Chancellor arrived in 1553, opening the way for world trade. It lost most of its vitality over the years until World War I, when it came back on the scene by becoming a huge warehouse for Allied supplies. "The war had changed Archangel to the extent that it became very much busier, for until Murmansk was completed, it remained Russia's only European port not blockaded by the Germans. . . . On its quays were piled the supplies and armaments bought abroad by the Tsarist government on war credits from the Allies. . . ."[92] The Railroads and warehouses could not cope with all the supplies that were piled for future use. Many items went unpacked and just piled high.[93] Archangel had virtually only one product that was exported, timber, and it all went to Britain. Lenin surmised this was another reason for the British intervention in his country: "This region of European Russia has served in this respect as an external market for Britain without being an internal market for Russia."[94] Lenin felt it was a one way street. Russian timber was being sucked out of the country without proper compensation.

The climate of the area was harsh. The summer heat was tropical with swampy mosquito marshes. Winter brought the Arctic air, with two hours of daylight and temperatures rarely above minus 30 degrees centigrade. The White Sea was frozen most of the year, so Archangel was often ice-locked for several months. In some areas the railroads could only be used in the winter, as the frozen tundra supported the weight of the trains that the summer swamps could not.

In December of 1917, the British had been guarding the vast quantity of ammunition and equipment at Archangel, when they received orders to leave. They would leave the supplies unprotected while they proceeded to Murmansk, as ordered. The British government offered to send shipments of food and medicine to Archangel if the local populace would keep the stockpiles from falling into the hands of the Bolsheviks, and if need be, away from the Germans. This area had substantial timber, therefore, the British also wanted to keep an influence in the area. Unfortunately, the Bolsheviks captured the city on February 10, 1918. Archangel needed to be retaken. With the help of a local coup on July 31 that brought in a friendly government, the British, under Major General Frederick C. Poole, with a small army of about 1,500 men, re-entered the city without bloodshed. Poole was a very aggressive officer and wrote, "I am quite cheerfully taking great risks." There is no indication that Poole ever knew of the restrictions President Wilson had stipulated for the conduct of Allied intervention.[95] Poole was about to start a "thoroughly aggressive campaign."

As the American troops arrived they were handed a pamphlet, written by the British, describing the situation in the region. Its description of the Bolsheviks was as follows: "The Bolshevik is a criminal who is fighting because order means defeat for his regime. He sees a rope around his neck for his past misdeeds . . . . The

German will appear in Russian uniform and can not be distinguished from the rest. The Bolshevik is controlled by Germany and is to be opposed."[96] This, it can be surmised, was to show the "Sammies" why they were in Russia. The British had very little regard for the Russians, as the document continued by saying the Russian people were "curious and inquisitive," and should be "treated like a child."

"We unloaded the boat [landing in Russia] and [the next day] I was on the front line fighting." Cpl. Colburn recalled later skirmishes: "They [Bolsheviks] were hiding behind trees that were cut off and [the Bolsheviks would] take a few steps toward us. Then they would wait and take a few more steps at a time. And that's the way we fought them."[97] One part of his handwritten diary reads: "Up and stood to at 3 bells. Expected attack on account of Bolo shooting star shells. First Bolo spied by Pvt. Stemzyk at about 7:40. Directly Pvt. Kroenkie shouted oh, god here comes a 1000,000 [sic]. I ordered windowes [sic] raised. Gunner Minteer on Lewis gun opened first then enemy. Then I cut loose with old Vic. Steady exchange of fire for 1 1/4 hrs. straight . . . Pvt. Becker and I about kissed ourselves goodby. Becker's pill passed just over his head & went out our back door & mine hit my tripod directly in front of me. . . ."[98] The soldiers were never told of President Wilson's orders, so they obeyed orders as good soldiers do. Many officers would later remark how exceptional these soldiers were.

Right from the beginning, "It was a botched job if there ever was one."[99] The Polar Bears arrived in Russia and were immediately sent to the front. One British officer in command of the Allied troops set the tone as soon as the Americans landed: "'All patrols must be aggressive, and it must be impressed on all ranks that we are fighting an offensive war, and not a defensive one.' Possibly it was the grotesque gap between this order and President Wilson's policy of peaceful intervention in North Russia that was responsible for the odd behavior of the American commanding officer. . . . He had not yet been officially posted on that policy, but many American officials in Archangel knew of it, and he must have been generally aware of the chasm between American theory and British practice."[100] As these orders were given to the Americans, the British were pulled back to guard the stockpiles. This seemed to set the stage for an immediate moral problem against the British. Animosity quickly built toward them. Besides being forced to exchange clothing, they were given unfamiliar weapons, put under command of British officers, told to fight against an unknown foe for an unknown cause, and then the ultimate degradation took place – the American flag was not allowed to be brought to Russia (see footnote).[101]   When the Americans arrived in Archangel, Russia, they were met by the President of the North Russian government, Nicholas V. Tschaikovsky. He was holding in his hands what he perceived to be an American flag. The Polar Bears at first thought it was the new flag of the North Russian government, as the stripes ran north and south. The Americans decided to paint a facsimile on gates or fences or any other place to distinguish themselves from the others. The British did not want this to be done and wanted only the Union Jack shown. American pride and ingenuity prevailed: "Members of Company H, who had been wounded or otherwise incapacitated, found an imperial Russian flag in the barracks in which they were recuperating. The colors were right, white, red and blue. So they tore it into strips to make an American flag. I painted stars in the flag."[102] Many soldiers wrote home reflecting their feelings toward the British. "Here. . .are scores of officers (mostly British...) who are perjured again and again; liars, whore-mongers, booze-fighting, who absolutely fear to venture near the front, much less under fire, knowing certainly that a well deserved bullet in the back would be the messenger of justice."[103] The British seemed to be the easiest target to vent the anger generated by a cruel, bitter campaign of miserable weather, long terrible nights and inadequate food. "We are getting dirty stunts pulled on us all the time by the low down English. We can't help it, got no one to back us up if Limeys get into any kind of a scrape . . . they call us up (to fight the English battles for them). . . . The Russians have no use for the English. I haven't seen anybody yet that did."[104]   It should be noted that other complaints, besides about the British, were made.

One veteran complained that the ice got so thick on the rivers that trains could run over it. Another soldier told the story of just arriving in Russia and being attacked not only from the front but the enemy somehow got behind them: "[We] turned cannon around setting it at zero and let Bolos have it! 300 are killed."[105]

The British "aggressive" behavior led to the first American combat deaths.

Two platoons of Company I, under Lieutenant Gordon B. Reese, somehow got separated from the rest of the battalion and soon ran completely out of ammunition. Reese then demonstrated a tough Yankee spirit by ordering a bayonet charge instead of retreat or surrender. The Bolsheviks had not expected this, and themselves retreated in dismay before the yelling *Amerikanskis,* who were then able to work back to the main body of the battalion.

Two members of Company I, however, and one of Company L, were found dead in the woods after the fight was over. It was not yet two weeks since they had marched off the troop ship at Archangel. They were buried beneath wooden crosses at Obozerskaya, two boys from Detroit and one from Pittsburgh who had come a long way to die, for reasons that were by no means clear.[106]

Colonel Stewart added to his deteriorating popularity by not attending this funeral nor any other funeral during his stay in Russia. In fact, he never visited the front lines. He stayed in his quarters most of the time it is now surmised, because of his lack of authority – All British officers outranked all the other Allied officers.[107] ". . . Colonel Stewart and his headquarters staff gave the impression of being both cowed by the British and strangely disinterested in the problems of the fighting fronts. . . . He knew that he stood in constant violation of President Wilson's orders. . . . The Americans in from the front, however, knew nothing of all this, and to them Stewart's behavior was unforgivable."[108]

The British and French continued to request more troops from the United States, despite what Wilson had said in his *Aide Memoire*. They felt five more battalions of American troops were needed to succeed. President Wilson, Secretary of State Lansing and General March decided against any additional troops. Lansing cabled Francis to inform him of the decision the next day:

It is the opinion of this government that there is no hope of gathering any effective force of Russians. We shall insist to other governments that all activities in North Russia be abandoned except for guarding military stores. You will be cut off as Archangel becomes ice-locked. Supplies will go to Murmansk. No more troops will be sent to the northern ports.[109]

This decision would force the Americans to do what the original orders demanded to be on the defensive. Unfortunately for the "Polar Bears," it also signaled that they would be on their own for survival. Should the Bolsheviks start a major offensive against them, the Americans could not expect reinforcements, and total annihilation was certain.

Washington felt the western front was too important to spare any soldier. If need be, the Russian contingent would have to be sacrificed.

In Russia, the mood was getting worse. Only American and French forces were used on the front lines with no British forces sent for reinforcements. Francis requested that an "American General in command would have good effect . . . .British are hated . . . ."[110] Francis could see that the English officers had inflicted low morale among the Americans.

In October, a change was made. General Edmund Ironside replaced General Poole. Ironside was thirty-eight years old and could speak Russian along with six other languages. He found Poole's command in complete shambles. Records were missing, no general staff and, unbelievably, no maps of any troop movements.[111] This astonishing discovery gave great credence to the complaints of the Americans. Ironside's arrival did decrease the friction, somewhat, between the soldiers. He was honest and forthright with all of his officers. During an operation on January 3, poor performance by a British commander cost eight American soldiers their lives. The first reports placed the blame on the Russian regiment that failed to support the Americans. General Ironside determined that the British officer in command was to blame, as he was found to be intoxicated. The British officer was court-martialed.[112] Within a few weeks of Ironside's arrival, however, November 11, 1918, news arrived that an armistice had been signed in Paris between the Allies and Germany. No longer would Allied military stores need to be protected from Germany and no longer would the eastern front need to be reestablished. The War was over and everyone began the thoughts of coming come – except those in Russia. World euphoria was produced by the end of the bloodiest conflict the world had ever seen. It is easy to see how the conflict in Russia was overshadowed. Most Americans did not know that the Russian expedition had even taken place. Their thoughts and prayers, similar to the American government, centered on the soldiers in France.

The Allied governments began organizing the peace conference when Winston Churchill insisted that another evil was still around – Bolshevism. He wanted the Allies to continue the fight and would later say, "The day will come when it will be recognized without doubt throughout the civilized world that the strangling of Bolshevism at birth would have been an untold blessing to the human race."[113] British General Sir Henry Wilson told the British War Cabinet that the Allies had three choices in Russia: withdraw all forces and build a ring of states to contain Bolshevism; crush the Bolsheviks; or give assistance to the White Army in Russia and withdraw Allied troops. The United States had to decide on one of those choices or simply withdraw and let the Russia people decide their own fate. It was decided to let the troops remain in Russia until the peace talks commenced in mid-January. Not making a decision was easier then making one. Unfortunately, the Polar Bears were left in limbo.

The fighting from the war stopped around the world, except in Russia. Fierce battles raged in North Russia between the Allies and Bolsheviks and would last through May of 1919, long after the armistice had been signed. One American soldier wrote, "On Armistice Day our outpost. . . are attacked at dawn. Three days and three nights follow. Many are killed."[114] Fighting in a land that defied description, and doing so after the Armistice was signed was too much for some to accept. They asked, "Why [are] only American and French are allowed on the actual firing line? Why [are] all American flags requested to be turned into British ordinance? Why [do] the Royal Engineers never go into the field? Why are we fed English rations and officered by English officers?"[115] Morale was so bad that some French troops mutinied. There were even stories, circulating at the time, of an American mutiny and of an American sergeant ending his life by putting a revolver to his head. However, the American mutiny never happened, even though it played in the American newspapers at home; and the sergeant killed himself after being accused of cowardice. [116]

The soldiers lamented in their predicament: "But the days, deadly and monotonous, followed. . . there was no promise of relief, no word, no news of any kind, except the stories of troops returning home from France. Doubtless in the general hilarity over peace, we were forgotten. After all, who had time in these world stirring days to think of an insignificant regiment performing in a fantastic Arctic side show."[117]

Cleo Colburn related how the biggest battle he fought came after the Armistice, "Well, my squad was in a block house and our guard out front came in and said Corporal, I see motion out in the woods. So I told everybody to stand-to and I was operating a Vickers gun [machine gun] and the boys were operating a Lewis gun [machine gun] and we had an hour and fifteen minutes of steady fire fighting. Finally we got French Artillery and that rolled them back. They dropped a bomb on one rear corner and then the next and we were sure they got us! We thought it was the Bolos. I can't tell you how many [men] were lost but it was a number. We didn't lose anybody but a lot of Bolos died."[118]

The battle that took place on November 11 and carried on until the 14th, was known as "The Battle of Armistice Day." The fighting was centered around a small village called Tulgas, about two hundred miles southeast of Archangel. American losses were 28 dead and many more wounded. Bolshevik dead were counted on the field at four hundred.[119] (Some reports recorded three hundred killed.) The American force could have easily been decimated by Bolshevik forces, but the "Bolos" did not mount a full-scale attack on the retreating Americans.[120]

Why they did not attack is left unanswered. Were the Bolsheviks fully defeated and demoralized as many accounts give or did Leon Trotsky hold back the complete annihilation of the Americans for fear of a total commitment by Washington? According to Bolshevik prisoners taken, Trotsky himself directed the operation, traveling in his famous armored train taking day to day command. The prisoners said that Trotsky watched the fighting from one of the river gunboats.[121]

The Bolsheviks were a determined people. Although disorganized at first, the communists quickly regrouped. The "Red Army" commanded by Commissar

Trotsky eventually fielded 18 armies. The Bolshevik armies' official emblem, a five pointed red star with hammer and plow, became a familiar sight to the Americans.[122] The American doughboys both feared and admired the Russian troops. The feeling was mutual as the 82nd Tarasovo Regiment even refused to face American riflemen whom they called "fiends." They threatened to shoot their commissars if they were forced once again to fight the 339th.[123]

The Russians were a hardened lot. Their ways were uncivilized to Americans, both in fighting or in life in general. The Americans became disgusted with even the friendly Russian soldiers in camp, as one American, (serious intent, but humorous nevertheless), wrote that "instead of using seats as all civilized people do, [these] oafs . . . squatted over the seats and deposited their excretion on the seats. Even more disgusting was their filthy habit of using their fingers instead of the toilet paper provided and wiping them off on the newly painted walls. . . ."[124]

The Bolsheviks also fought with unknown tenaciousness and brought fear to the Americans. Many of the Americans heard what happened to one of their units when they were surrounded and fighting like "Custer at Little Big Horn." All the Americans were killed. When their bodies were recovered the next day, there was a ring of the enemy dead all around them attesting to the ferocity of their last stand. There was a special funeral ceremony for Lieutenant Cliff: "We were lined up in the street in front of our barracks, the Captain (Kinjon) made a short speech. The enemy, he said, were castrating the wounded while they were still alive, when Lieutenant Cuff pulled out his revolver and shot himself. This is the 'kind of enemy you are fighting,' he concluded."[125] Cuff's body was mutilated before the Americans could reach him. His body was returned and buried at White Chapel Cemetery on May 30, 1930. The incident served as an effective means to rally the troops against the enemy.

The American troops spearheaded the drives on every front and were usually the most exposed units. The Yanks were strung out over 200 miles from Archangel, and as far south as Shnkeursk. The only way to get the wounded to the rear was by sleds pulled by reindeer. "Week follows week and November goes by, and December, and no word comes from the War Department," recorded Lt. Cudahy, a future American Ambassador. "No word comes, and the soldier is left to think that he has been abandoned by his country and left to rot on the barren snow wastes of Arctic Russia."[126]

By the end of 1918, there were approximately 13,000 Allied troops in North Russia, including Americans, British, French, Serbs, Canadians, Italians, Australians, Finns and a small number of Chinese.[127] There were six fronts, totaling almost five hundred miles. This was an extremely small size force to be in such a large area.

Morale was getting worse. The harsh winter and thoughts of American troops arriving home from France was taking a toll on the Americans in this far away land. "Not only had it [America] committed several thousands of its soldiers to a military involvement on Russian soil which had now lost what rationale it might once have had and which could not, in the circumstances, have been more confused, more futile, or more misleading, but it had sacrificed to this dubious undertaking the slender thread of communication with the new government in Russia. . . . and never, surely, in the history of American diplomacy has so much been paid for so little."[128]

As the fighting escalated with furious abandonment, it became psychologically debilitating, not only for the warriors on the field but also for the families at home.

❋

CHAPTER III

DETROIT'S REACTION

How much longer is the blood of Michigan boys to stain the snows
of north Russia?

–Mrs. George Garton

For God's sake say something and do something!
– Detroit's Own Welfare Assoc.

The world rejoiced that the war was over. The boys would be returning home
from France. It had been a long and bloody conflict, but it was time to heal and
become "human" again. It was time to march in a parade, handshake a civil war vet,
and think about the future that seemed so bright. Americans were proud of their
accomplishment to end all wars. For most, life was returning to normalcy, although
not for everyone. The Americans in Russia did not come home. Had America
forgotten them? December brought Christmas joy to the homes of millions, but
many Michigan homes were quiet. For them, instead of celebration, it was a time of
solemn prayers. On December 25, instead of headlines that read, "Merry Christmas,"
Michigan papers proclaimed "Detroit's Own Fights On." Lists of the dead and
wounded were on the front pages and the stories of bravery continued to be reported.
The war did not end for these Michigan men, nor did it end for the wives and parents
of these soldiers. Michiganders were not able to rejoice as the rest of the world was
rejoicing. The privilege to celebrate the ending of the war was not yet theirs.

In January and February of 1919, Michigan families were reading articles of
men and women returning from France with their stories of thrills and many chills.

A story on the front page of a Michigan paper told of the return of "Eddie" Rickenbacker and of his honors and the exciting "adventure" he had during the war. But the main headline was about another story, "Reds Drive Allies Back 40 Miles."[129]

Another article quoted the story of a "Detroit's Own" soldier: "We never took any prisoners. Orders from the British commander were read to the company saying that they didn't want to be bothered with any prisoners. So when one of the Bolsheviki came out of his lines with his hands over his head, he was either shot by us or by his own officers."[130]

The beginning of February also brought stories of political intrigue: "Republicans Launch Fight On Wilson;" but Detroiters read headlines in local newspapers that announced, "339th Suffers Heavy Losses," and "Reds Threaten to Encompass Allies on Dvina."[131] The families worried; the country seemed to be carrying on as if all was well, but all was not well, at least not in Michigan.

The first report of any protest movement was made on February 2.

Many disturbing reports continued to trickle in from Russia that seemed to spell doom for the Americans. "Washington Is Fearful of Disaster Near Archangel," read one headline. In this article, the last paragraph called for the families to unite,

> . . . Relatives of men fighting with 'Detroit's Own' in northern Russia plan a mass meeting of protest Monday night in Trinity church, northeast corner of Trumbull avenue and Myrtle street, and then will circulate a petition to Congress demanding the immediate withdrawal. . . .Copies of this petition may be obtained after today by persons wishing to circulate them from the office of Dr. Allan L. Richardson. . . . It is hoped to obtain 250,000 signatures.[132]

Newsmen were present at the meeting in Trinity Church on February 3. The next day the editor of the *Detroit News* wrote that in answer to the plea from the parents of the boys of the 339th, the *News* would contact   Jay G. Hayden,[133] staff correspondent at the peace conference in France. On February 4, Hayden spoke directly to President Wilson to learn the exact status of the Detroiters at Archangel, and reported back to the newspaper of his meeting with the President.   This interview was a well documented and detailed analyses of the situation; and was later read on the floor of Congress. It reported the honorable intentions of the President when first sending the troops to Russia and also reflected on the candid inner struggles that took place within the Administration about this decision. According to Hayden, the tone of the meeting was serious as the President tried to answer questions from the parents' meeting, such as, the slowness of the casualty list report and the nonexistent communication between soldier and family. He was also asked about why the soldiers were still in Russia and when they would be coming home? "The force which is holding the little band of Allied troops," Hayden wrote, "including Detroit's own regiment, in the heart of Northern Russia, in a position of unquestioned serious danger, is a combination of Arctic weather and diplomatic exigency."   Hayden further reported that it was doubtful that the troops would be removed any time soon. He was told there were political problems that were in a "tangle of considerations in international relations with which the whole Russian problem is enmeshed."   He was also told by the President that the American government was not ignoring the plight of Archangel soldiers and that "Col. House is devoting his whole time right now to the specific problem and Glen. Bliss also is giving it much attention." The President insisted that the lists of casualties were not being withheld but delayed due to poor communications with the Russian field offices. The communication problem also resulted in few letters reaching home.

President Wilson was very candid in his comments. He believed the troops could continue to resist the Bolsheviks until spring, "Then it is admitted there may be great danger." Reinforcements were impossible, according to the President, because of the weather and the lack of troops in the area.

The reporter did other interviews which led to startling comments that were disconcerting to the family members: "The history of the Russian intervention revealed to me by an American authority so high that it is beyond possibility to question its accuracy, shows the position of the troops. . . to be the result of one of the worst possible policy blunders of the war." The American President was in favor of withdrawing all the troops as soon as possible, but it was a "diplomatic necessity of a continued harmonious relation with the Allies . . . ." that would stall any movement. It seemed to the love ones that politics was keeping the troops in Russia. The President went on to explain the purpose of the expedition: because of the fall of the Russian government the Allied cause was in great danger. "Germany was withdrawing 60 divisions from the east to the west front and Allied authorities were united in the opinion they could not hold the French front (for long). . . . "

A plan had been presented to the Allies (Wilson does not say by whom) to invade in sufficient strength to reestablish the eastern front. The Americans were against an invasion primarily because of the extreme difficulties of transporting a large army across Siberia. However, a modified intervention was agreed to, which would include an American landing at Murmansk and Archangel, "for the exclusive purpose of guarding supplies." The United States agreed to turn the command over to the British because the American contingent would be defensive in nature. The British would be on the direct lines and the Americans would guard the supplies. Great Britain was also assuring the White House that, "the Russians were for Allied intervention and that if given aid a large Russian army could be recruited against the Bolshevik." According to an unnamed source, the plan was to easily recruit a 100,000 man Russian army on the Allied side. In reality, the total would reach only

5,000 and their reliability was questioned. This would be reflected in the Shenkursk Battalion (reported later in this chapter).

The reporter quoted American sources that tended to blame the British for the situation: "The opinion was expressed to me by one very high American official. . . [the] expeditions were never more than a cloak to hide the real aim, which was to force the Allies into active warfare against the Bolsheviki. It is well known that at this time there was great pressure from British and French interests for strong intervention in Russia. A little army in the far interior of Russia in great danger naturally would demand reinforcements, and soon a complete state of war would be brought about and it is quite conceivable this plan would have succeeded but for the armistice, which changed the whole aspect of the Russian situation by eliminating the element of the German threat."

In other words, the top goal of the Allies (other than the United States, it seems) was to eliminate the Bolshevik regime and then worry about a second front. Had the war continued, Americans could scarcely have refused the steps necessary to protect their troops. Hayden reported that conferences were in progress with the British and French on how to withdraw from the area and leave the internal affairs to the Russian people, however, "There is grave doubt now if the meeting will be successful."

Finally in February, one of the first reported comments about the Polar Bears was made by Representative Mason, a Republican Congressmen from Illinois. It was none too loud as it came at the end of a statement he made on U.S. interest in Russian bonds. Almost as an afterthought he said, "There is no reason for American boys to sacrifice their lives in Russia today. We are apparently opposing Soviet. Are we supporting Czarism and the restoration of militarism and imperialism to Russia? It looks that way."[134]

About 2,000 relatives and friends of the Polar Bears arrived at another meeting at the Trinity Church as was reported by the local media on February 5. The plans were set to demand the recall of the soldiers using petitions that would be circulated. The group was officially formed and called "Detroit's Own Welfare" with an executive committee which included: Edmund Christian, Charles Ginsberg, Theodore D. Hall, R.S. Hartill, O. Webster Kay, Frank L. Meyers, John T. Paine, Frank Puddeford, Dr. A.L. Richardson, A. Smart and D. P. Stafford. Dignitaries also showed their support by attending or sending letters of affirmation. "Theodore D. Hall, chairman, announced the purpose of the meeting, and Dr. James W. Inches, police commissioner, said that Mayor Couzens heartily favored the proposed action. A letter from Governor Sleeper also expressed sympathy."[135] The meeting was orderly but their resolve was evident. Loud applause constantly interrupted speakers. It was also very important to friends and family members that no dishonor come to the soldiers. "Mrs. J. Brooks Nichols, wife of Major Nichols, of the 339th, urged that nothing be done to embarrass the regiment. 'We want them brought out of danger of massacre,' she said, 'but not as Detroit's Own quitters.'"[136] Another article with a similar theme had a headline that read, "Don't Make Quitters of 339th, Major's Wife Asks."[137] These were very patriotic Americans who only wanted answers to their questions. They did not want their loved ones home if it brought disgrace to them or to the United States. Other articles appeared throughout February and the headlines were similar: "339th Again In Battle; Citizens Demand Recall."[138] Later in February, the Association met again at the Calvary Presbyterian Church. The headline read, "339th Parents Wire Wilson."[139] This would be the first "official" meeting of the newly formed "Detroit's Own Welfare Association." "The . . . Association wired President Wilson this morning requesting a public declaration of the Administration's attitude toward the American troops in North Russia. A resolution determining this course was unanimously carried at a meeting of the newly-organized association." The second meeting became very emotional. "Handkerchiefs were in evidence" as the emotions came to the surface, particularly when D.P. Stafford read a long account of the interview between Detroit's committee and Secretary Baker in Washington on February 15. Mr. Baker freely admitted that life on the Russian front ". . . was uncomfortable, but differed from the committee's view that troops were not obligated to serve after Germany's retirement from the war, and could offer no comfort. . . ." The Association was simply asking for an answer to the question, "Why were the men still there since the Germans had been defeated and the war had ended?

Many in the crowd wept and were comforted by others. The meeting then endorsed the articles of association. "The purpose of the association will be to use every legitimate means to have the American forces in Russia withdrawn or reinforced and, after their return, to perform welfare work while there is need for it." Since so many of the soldiers were now returning to the United States from Europe, many sought after jobs were disappearing. It was obvious (so they thought) there would be lines for jobs, and the Polar Bears would be at the ends of those lines. The Association was keenly aware of this possible scenario and wanted the homecoming to be joyous and worry free as possible. "Financial plans were laid for helping the returned men to employment, civilian clothes, and whatever individual cases may require. . . ." The aims of the organization were reiterated by the chairman, R.S. Hartill, so that it would be reported that it did not have an anti-United States agenda nor was it meant to be politically oriented. The loyalty to America was expressed over and over again.

Hartill "reiterated its loyalty and repudiated any sympathy with Bolshevism. He spoke warmly of the assistance given his committee by the Michigan delegation at the capital and acknowledged the efforts of Sen. Hiram Johnson of California. Not only Detroit but all of Michigan is showering protest on Washington, and the resolution finally adopted requesting an avowal from the President is sent in an effort to obtain a definite statement."

The State Senate demanded action: "A demand that the 339th Infantry and other American troops be removed from command of foreign officers and immediately withdrawn from Russia was unanimously passed by the senate Wednesday in the form of a resolution. 'If the Archangel expedition ever had a valid excuse, it cannot now be justified, either on the ground of military expediency or of humanity. . . there is no patriotic reason why our American soldiers in Russia should not have at least an equal chance for their lives with other American soldiers.'"[140]

Senators outside the state were beginning to express their concern in Washington. Besides Representative Mason of Illinois, Senator Johnson of California expressed his outrage by bringing the Michigan resolution to the attention of the full Senate. "Senator Johnson and others inquiring the whys and wherefores of the little group of American soldiers in the heart of Arctic Russia."[141] Johnson proposed a resolution to withdraw all Americans from Russia immediately. The vote was taken and the outcome was reported in the newspaper the next day, "Senate Blocks Action On Russian Withdrawal."[142] The Senator "was blocked in attempting to get consideration for his resolution on the withdrawal of American troops from Russia in the Senate this afternoon. . . ."

In Northern Russia, the solders continued to fight for survival with uncertain Allies. The Americans were making a retreat from Shenkursk and left the Shenkursk Battalion to guard the rear, keeping the enemy from getting too close. The Shenkursk Battalion was an entirely Russian unit, mobilized from local villages. Upon their engagement with the Bolsheviks, "two entire companies went over to the

Bolo side" leaving the rest of the unit to flee or be killed. The "Bears" struggled through large drifts of snow and extreme bitter cold as they fled for their survival. "Time after time that night one could hear some poor unfortunate with his heavy pack on his back fall with a sickening thud upon the packed trail."[143] Other reports were coming from wounded vets who arrived back in the United States. One such veteran was First Sergeant Dorsey Payne of Detroit. He was with Company I, of the 339th Infantry and was wounded in the left hip. He brought back "vivid" stories of the fighting taking place. Payne said there were times the men would go as long as three days without food, and were fighting continuously. Just before being wounded, Payne recalled, the Bolsheviks made a charge on their position and "the Americans opened up with their machine [guns] and automatic guns and mowed them down, leaving 500 dead or wounded out of 1,000."[144] Stories like these caused fear and anger to rise in Michigan.

The Michigan people continued to write to Washington, their Senators, and to the newspapers, with even more determination. They did not want their boys to simply disappear and never to be heard from again. This concern for "disappearing" was real to the families as evidenced by a letter written by Mrs. Mark Smith from Armada, Michigan. It was to the editor of the *Detroit News,* telling of the letter she wrote to the Adjutant-General asking the whereabouts of her husband who was with the 339th. The reply indicated he was in good health and stationed in Toul, France! "This," she stated, "is proof that government officials know nothing of our boys in Russia. Of course, they can't know why they are fighting, for no one does. How long must we people of this democratic land stand for this?" Other letters, outside of Michigan, began to appear: "How much longer is the blood of Michigan boys to stain the snows of north Russia," writes Mrs. George Garton, of St. Louis Mo., "What is wrong with the Michigan representatives in Washington? Have they nothing to say on the subject? I read The Free Press (newspaper) daily and I fail to see what they have done, though The Free Press has worked faithfully for the troops' withdrawal." Letters and poems were flowing into Washington:

What About Bringing Them Home?

Did we declare war upon Russia?
When we took a hand in the game
I know that we hopped onto Prussia,
And Austria got it the same.
But still I have no recollection,
Of breaking with Russia, I swear,
And cannot help making objection,
To having our boys over there.

What quarrel have we with that nation?
Just how did it tread on our toes?
We prate of our friendly relation,
Then how can we class them as foes?
I'll back up most any complete fight,
So long as we really make war,
But this is too much like a street fight,
And nobody knows what it's for.

I know that a red reign of terror
Is flaming throughout Russia today,
But still I insist it an error
To bring Yankee troops into play.
We wound up the big war in Europe,
We settled the major campaign,
Then why should they ask us to cure up
The festers that seem to remain?

It's Europe's own fight we are waging,
For we're at war with the Russ,
And what is the sense of engaging
In something that doesn't affect us?
Our own boys have tackled a struggle

That no one should ask them to bear.
Their lives are too precious to juggle,
Now, why are they fighting out there?

We say that the struggle is finished,
We say that the war has been won,
The army will soon be diminished.
The boys who demolished the Hun
To all of their home folks are writing,
"We'll soon be recrossing the foam."
Then why are these other boys fighting?
And, what about bringing them home?

–GEORGE L. SMITH.[145]

Finally, other newspapers from around the country began to report the Russian situation. In Chicago, the front page ran an article titled, "Allied Effort In Far North Series Of Ills - Errors, Jealousy and Fears Defeat All Their Intent."[146] The Chicago Tribune investigated the conditions in Russia and began to report a series of articles that were "uncovering a number of facts." These reports were carried by other newspapers around the country. The facts centering on the failed effort, were these: (1) There was a great deal of mistrust and animosity between the Allied armies, especially between the British and others. The in-fighting had lessened the effectiveness of the effort to help the Russians. (2) The American troops were put under the command of another country. This action was completely contrary to the tradition of the United States Armed Forces. "They were put to doing a King's business . . . American men and their ideals of right and fairness were entirely submerged through the un-American leadership." (3) It was more a political fight rather than military, but the leadership had shown a great lack of diplomacy. (4) The expedition lacked a spiritual direction. The soldiers hated their jobs and despised the Russian people. "The expedition, lacking this spiritual significance in men's minds, has become a mere fighting job to collect Russia's debt to Europe." (5) The friendly

Russians did not have any enthusiasm to help the Allies in fighting the Bolsheviks. The Russians themselves had "a growing disgust against the expedition, especially against the British." (6) Within our own forces, the Americans lacked leadership that would stop some of the abuses.

The author, Frazier Hunt, further expressed his contempt for the entire situation as he described the censorship that took place in Russia: "The American public has been fed pretty stories of the gentle glories of this 'Help Russia' expedition, but the facts are that a mess has been stewed and has been kept for the cooks themselves." He related that American sons were being sacrificed and that the American public should finally know what was taking place: Russians resented the interference in their affairs and desired the control of their personal and political lives. Hunt further reported that the Russian's resentment grew when they were considered Bolsheviks and thrown into jail for failing to follow an order by the Allied government. To make matters worse, Marshall Law was declared so that local governments were under military control. "Then into this boiling mess, is stuck a bayonet instead of a spoon, and this new outside foreign cook, whose recipes are not wanted, whose ability is questioned, whose sincerity is doubted shouts, 'Try my brand of cooking. You need it, try it, or I'll stick you with a bayonet.'"

Senator Johnson, on February 13, read the Tribune article to the Senate floor relating it as "the latest statement of fact from an eyewitness." After reading the report he lamented, "Our supineness, our cowardice, is risking 5,000 precious American lives in Russia without a plan, scheme or purpose." Johnson asked again for a vote to withdraw the troops. This began the spark that would ignite a full uproar in Congress. Senator Hitchcock, chairman of the foreign relations committee, objected to an immediate vote. "We expect to get out of Russia. It is the policy of the president to bring our soldiers out as soon as possible." He urged that a vote not be taken that would show disunity within the Congress on this important issue. The world, he continued, needed to see that our foreign policy under President Wilson was supported by the U. S. Congress. Republican Leader Henry C. Lodge spoke sharply against the intervention while Senator Lewis of Illinois, the Democratic whip, agreed with the President's decision.[147] Intermingled in the heated debate was a resolution presented by Michigan Senator Smith from the citizens of Grand Rapids, Michigan, "declaring against the retention of American troops in Russia and urging their withdrawal as soon as possible."[148] A vote was not taken and the day ended.

Heartbreaking letters continued to flood the newspapers from around the country. One such letter to the editor read: "We learn that . . . a petition is to be forwarded to Congress requesting the withdrawal of the American troops . . . . We received a letter from Washington telling us that Lieutenant Ralph Powers died on January 22 of wounds received in action. With aching hearts we realize that relief for the expedition is too late for our dear boy, but we would add our name to the petition for the sake of those who remain. . . in what appears to be a tragical blunder."[149]

February 14 and 15 brought further discord on the floor of Senate. A debate on the "rivers and harbor" bill was in progress, when Senator Johnson interrupted and asked for a motion to supplant that measure and proceed with consideration of his resolution. He was not to be denied. There was a brief debate with "Senator Sherman of Illinois, occupying most of the time in support of the resolution and denunciation of the Bolshevist regime in Russia. He also criticized administration policies." Senator McCumber of North Dakota, a Republican, declared that aid should be given to the "good people" [In Russia], to establish a stable government. Another Senator, Borah, shouted, "Do you contend that America should send to Russia from 250,000 to 500,000 soldiers and have them stay there until the Russians could establish a stable government?" McCumber shouted back, "No, but I would have them stay there long enough to get rid of Lenine and Trotsky." [150] Senator Fletcher of Florida, one of the Democratic leaders, moved to table the resolution. A vote was called to table. The result was 33 votes for and 33 votes against tabling. "Only the vote of Vice President Marshall, exercised for the first time this session, saved the administration forces in the Senate today from a serious defeat on the Russian policy. . . . Senator Johnson announced, however, that he would bring the measure up again in a day or two in a slightly different form, and would keep it before the Senate until it was voted on again." Senator Sherman gleefully announced he was glad for the vote and "I hope it will be kept up until the germ of bolshevism is completely destroyed."[151] This exchange between senators was reported in one Michigan newspaper next to a picture of Lieut. Clifford B. Ballard and the caption, "Detroit Officer Is Killed In Russia."

The same day, a Michigan delegation brought what the papers called, a "monster petition" of 105,000 signatures,[152] asking for the "recall or reinforcement of the American forces in Russia." There were no threats or demands – these were patriotic citizens who loved their country and only wanted fairness without any incriminations. This was also true of the soldiers themselves. They were told of the gallant effort by the "Detroit's Own Welfare," but they too were concerned for the integrity of the re-call mission. This was never more evident than by a letter sent from a "Polar Bear" to the editor of the *Detroit Free Press* newspaper. Lt. Lawrence P. Keith wrote: "Knowing the officers and men of the 339th Regiment as intimately as I do, I wish to say a word on their behalf, on behalf of the reputation of the regiment, and to correct certain erroneous ideas. . . . Some of our companies have undoubtedly gone through very severe hardships. . . . [however] I do not believe there is a member of the regiment that wants to be brought home on account of any hardships. We all know what Sherman said about war, and the real soldier takes that without crying or whimpering. Some of the men are having a very hard time. So did the men in the Argonne forest. The people of Detroit want these men returned, and the men will be only too glad to be brought back, and no one hopes that the government will consider this best more than I do. But, the whole regiment will want it done in a manner which they need not be ashamed of. Let the people of Detroit confine their arguments to the pros and cons of the necessity of keeping our men in that wilderness. We must remember that what hardships are there are unavoidable and we are not correcting any of them nor making it easier for the men by crying about it. Do not belittle the glory of our regiment by making the hardships the issue, but strive in such a way that when the men are brought back the city and soldiers will say with pride "Detroit's Own."[153] Keith spoke of ideals that were extremely important to many in 1919; glory yes, but even more so, reputation and pride.

The petitions were brought to Secretary Baker in the War Department, in Washington D. C. on February 15, by the Michigan delegation and also by a newly formed congressional delegation called "Detroit's Own." "This committee was named at the conference yesterday afternoon in the Ways and Means Committee room at the Capitol."[154] It consisted of Representatives Hamilton, Nichols, and Doremus of Michigan. The only disharmony came from another Michigan Representative at the meeting, citing "that all Michigan was interested and that the organization's title should be broadened to include the entire Wolverine state." The decision to keep the name without change was affirmed.

The delegation "heard little new from [him]," as the Secretary read from a prepared statement announcing only that, "assurance is given of [the] safety of [the] troops."[155] The *Free Press* editor replied with utter disbelief and disdain, "The disposition of the War Department to neglect our men in North Russia and evade any direct reply to pertinent questions concerning their situation is not to be considered for a moment with patience. Mr. Baker and his associates should be brought up with a round turn. So far as any plea that our soldiers are in care of the British war office and therefore out of Washington's control is concerned, the people of the United States certainly do not recognize any right of any foreign government to dispose of their troops over the head of the home government. When the American war department says it is helpless, it recognizes a British overlordship, and this is intolerable. The rising disposition of the Senate to take a hand in the matter is encouraging. We hope it will grow stronger until the administration is forced to act." Senator Johnson had stated earlier, "I will not for one instant concede that it is the duty of this republic to maintain order in a Jugo-Slav, Czecho-Slav or any other new state. I am opposed to American boys policing Europe and quelling riots in every nation's backyard."[156]

At the Russian front, the Bolsheviks were trying to take advantage of the disharmony. Leaflets were distributed in English throughout the area, calling upon the American soldiers to organize and demand that they be brought home. The announcement said that three million Bolshevik men would soon be ready to join the fight against the Americans. It further commented how the war with Germany was over, "and there is no reason for remaining in Russia."[157] Finally, a ray of hope – an article, dated February 14, was printed in *The Detroit News* with headlines, "339th Coming Home." It read "Assurance that the 339th infantry will not remain much longer in Russia was given Congressman Doremus of Detroit by Gen. Peyton C. March, Chief of Staff, today." General March said the matter of returning the Michigan boys home had been presented to the President, who was in Paris, and "there was every reason for believing that the necessary order directing the regiment's return will be issued...."[158] This was the first positive statement the families heard.

Still, no date for the evacuation was made, but were the political problems (the families had no idea what these political problems were) resolved? Two days later, more good news arrived.

The first actual time frame of a possible withdrawal was mentioned by Secretary Baker on February 17. He told the news media that all the American soldiers should be out of Russia by the spring. Large bold headlines read "339th Waits Recall."[159] It was not an exact date of departure, nor comments that would lead to joy in Detroit homes; but it was a thread of hope that the families grabbed. A "Letter to the Editor" by Colonel Stewart, the Commanding Officer of the 339th in Russia, seemed to confirm the spring departure: "We are closed in by ice until spring . . . . Request this [information] be given to the press and especially to Detroit and Chicago papers to allay any unnecessary anxiety."[160] After reading Mr. Baker's comments, Senator Johnson commented with some frustration, "When . . . we commenced the agitation, for the return of our troops in Russia for the sole purpose of saving the lives of American boys there, we had little sympathy and less support. After. . . absolute silence on the part of the Government, the denial of information of any sort either to Congress or to the people, comes today's communication, the first of its kind, to the military committees, that our soldiers would be returned. The strangeness of this communication does not detract from my very great gratification."[161]

But to the dismay and horror of many, the voices to remain in Russia were still being shouted. Roger E. Simmons, who had recently returned from a mission to Russia for the Bureau of Commerce, told the Senate Investigating Committee that if the American and Allied forces were withdrawn from northern Russia, "The Bolsheviki would engage in one of the bloodiest massacres the world has ever seen."[162] The *Detroit Journal* blasted his statement: "Mr. Simmons is only a minor official. . . . To the people of this state, the fighting in the Archangel region lacks excuse. . . . We doubt if Mr. Simmons has been sent over to the Capitol Hill to speak for the Administration. We suspect, from his words, that he rather speaks for those people who, while hating the Bolsheviki as most of us do, haven't the nerve to volunteer to fight these pests and want others to do the fighting for them.[163]

The "Star-Spangled Banner" was sung at the beginning of the Detroit's Own Welfare Association meeting on Friday, February 28. Many attended as they were again informed of the Association's determined effort to bring their boys back home. The Association would again wire President Wilson requesting a public declaration of the Administration's attitude toward the American troops in North Russia. After all the reports were given and prayers made, the session ended by singing, "My Country 'Tis of Thee."[164]

Fear still permeated many letters written home. Forty degrees below zero tended to numb the mind and also the will to keep hoping. "We would march a day, wet to the skin, and then have to sleep in our wet clothing. . . . It was worse when we were on outpost duty. We could not have fires, you knew if you moved, snipers would pick you off."[165] Bitterness toward the British continued to mount as the days stretched into weeks and months. John Dalian wrote home, "I hope some day the people in the States get the real story and the truth about this awful [situation]. . . . We are getting dirty stunts pulled on us all the time by the low down English. . . . They call us up to fight the English battles for them. . . . The Russians have no use for the English. I haven't seen anybody yet that did."[166] Corp. John W. Czerwinski wrote to his fiancé, "Never in my life was I ashamed of being an American until now, and I have to be because I know the Britons are putting something over on us."[167]

The family members turned the calendar page to March and still received no definitive word of the soldiers' return. Headlines continued to keep Michiganders informed and fearful, "Northern Horrors Give 339th Men New Disease;" "Allies Inflict Losses On Reds;" "Reds' Drive on 339th Blocked;" [168] Corp. Joseph J. Babinger wrote a letter to his brother that was published in the local papers saying, "Don't know how long we can hold out. Will fight to finish until help arrives."[169] Some, like Babinger, believed that help for them would come too late. Their hopes were beginning to dwindle.

Secretary of War Newton D. Baker made a visit to the home of the Polar Bears, Fort Custer, Battle Creek, Michigan on March 10. He announced that he was making every effort to have the 339th withdrawn from Russia at the earliest possible moment. He also stated that he would leave the latter part of the month for France and then travel to Russia for a firsthand look. This was very good news for the loved ones, but like a roller coaster, optimism brought realism when the families read the headlines on March 13, "339th And Allies Fall Back Again Before Reds - Bolsheviki Meet Heavy Losses On the Vaga Front." Another headline read, "Food Situation Grows Worse." Yet another, "1,000 of 5,000 Yanks In Northern Russia Are In 6 Hospitals." All of these startling headlines and a two month delay in getting mail from the front caused unbearable anxiety at home. Families were expressing their bitterness that their own government would allow this to happen.

April brought another outcry from Senator Johnson, "Five months have passed since the armistice – since we did the job for which America entered the war." He was incensed by the laissez-faire attitude of the American Government toward the dissipation of the troops and of the British Government for allowing the Americans to be used on the front lines. "Let's make it respectable to be American again," he lamented." He would start a new campaign beginning this date, April 4, 1919, with the slogan "America for America first." Johnson protested the idea that the President and "his court" were still in Europe finalizing the end of the war, when they should either be in Washington or Russia, finalizing the withdrawal of the only American troops that were still fighting. The Senator accused the President of neglecting American interests. The demoralized soldiers were asking only for justice, he said, while the future fate of America was being secretly debated in Paris. "Let's care for, guard, and protect our own. Bring American boys home, and let's be American again."[170]

The 5th of April brought the "second best" news possible. The soldiers were not coming home yet, but the time had been set! Headlines that day read, "339th Coming Home In June."[171] General March made an announcement in Washington, that the American forces in Russia would be heading home by the end of June. The waterways would be free of ice by that time and the soldiers would be transported to America. The family members slept better that night, but woke to the morning headlines that would churn their stomachs again, "Reds Cut 339th Infantry Lines - Bolshevik Loss 808, Allies 0, In Arctic Fight." Each day the families were presented with news of encouragement or reports that would bring them to new lows. Each day the tide in their own well being ebbed or flowed with the news media reports.

On the evening of April 7, the Association met and devised a stern letter to the President that was no longer asking , but demanding the return of the men. A cablegram was sent the next morning: "Relatives and friends of the United States soldiers in North Russia request their immediate withdrawal. One boat reached economic safety – others can. You already have announced troops will be withdrawn – cannot such action be taken at once? Direct answer expected. Signed: Detroit's Own Welfare Association." Boats had been arriving from Russia with the wounded. Why could they not transport the rest of the troops? The Association then sent a telegram to General Peyton C. March, chief of staff. It bitterly complained that the relatives were growing desperate and were not getting accurate information. For months, the letter continued, the Welfare Association had been endeavoring to obtain from the War Department a comprehensive report as to the situation of the 339th. Only vague answers had been received to quiet the anxiety of the relatives, aroused by repeated press dispatches and stories that were disconcerting. The letter desperately asked for his help before the "extermination of the regiment at the hands of the Bolsheviki or by disease" took place. The last sentence read, "For God's sake, say something and do something."[172] Panic and fear permeated the families. The thought that their own government had abandoned them, or at least was paralyzed into inaction, frightened them. Washington seemingly had put Russia's problems on hold, but the Polar Bears were not on hold; they kept fighting and dying.

April would also bring word back to the United States that one unit of the 339th had mutinied. It was also noted that many more of the Polar Bears were about to follow suit. If the people across the country and the government had not been concerned about the Russian operation, this revelation brought the matter to the forefront. Could it be possible that an American army unit had refused to fight? Newspaper after newspaper across the land picked up the first report by the Associated Press dated April 10, of the possible mutiny.[173] A few days later it was revealed that Company I of the 339th was the mutinous unit. Stories, editorials, and letters from citizens were published every day, either approving or condemning what took place. Many felt it was a black eye on Detroit. If nothing else, everyone became aware of the 339th in Russia. Even the Welfare Association asked for leniency for the mutineers. They met once again to form a letter to Provost Marshal Enoch Crowder stating that the Association would resent any harshness accorded to these troops. Unfortunately, it was not until the men arrived home did the truth prevail. An article was later published in the "Literary Digest" [174] that refuted the entire incident. The story began by saying that "Never was a more unjust charge laid against brave men. From the day they stepped off the boat. . . they were in the front line. . . with constant artillery fire, they were surrounded by a most exasperating condition." The article continued, "British, French, and Russian troops had mutinied. I talked today with dozens of men who witnessed them, both officer and enlisted men." Others had refused to fight but not the Americans. It was also noted that not a single word of the other mutinies got through the British censorship; only the false report about the Americans. The "Digest" explained that the Americans were ordered to take a position and refused. They requested to speak to their commander. Colonel Stewart appeared before the men and asked what the problem was. The men said they wanted to know why they were being sent, when "both the Russians and French were ready to take their turn, and also they wanted to know why they were fighting in Russia anyhow." The Colonel told them the Americans were fighting in Russia chiefly because they would be annihilated if they did not fight! No other answer was given so the men did what they were told to do. Corp. Cleo Colburn was a member of the I Company and his recollection of the incident was a little different: "Well, the French wouldn't go forward and we were detailed to take their place. And there was a Polish fellow who could not understand English very well. And he refused! Then, of course, talking to our Captain, he encouraged us to go and we obeyed. That's about all there was to this whole thing."[175]

Reports were beginning to appear in early May giving the indication that the Bolsheviks were massing forces in the area for a large scale offensive. Other reports, later declared untrue, made headlines with "60 American Soldiers Beheaded By Russian Axmen."[176] These and other stories kept the strain and dismay alive among the families. In Congress, a resolution asking for an explanation regarding the American troops in Russia was introduced on May 20 by Senator Poindexter, Republican from Washington; Representative Emerson, Republican from Ohio; and

Senator Johnson. They asked how many Americans were in Russia and for an explanation of the military policy being carried out.[177] Congress and the American people were being kept in the dark.

By the end of March, all French troops had been withdrawn from the front lines and American forces soon followed. Baker decided that an officer of higher rank was needed to command American forces; and, on April 14, General W.P. Richardson arrived in Archangel to take control of the American contingent. Richardson was to make preparations for the withdrawal of the Americans, which would take place as soon as spring had broken the frozen White Sea.[178] The newspapers heralded the good news; the boys would be home soon. Headlines read "339th To Sail Within Week," dated May 24. The Free Press was more accurate with "339th To See America Again On 4th Of July."[179]

American troops began their evacuation in late May, and by late June only a skeleton force remained. The war was finally over for these Michigan men. A total of 218 Americans had died, and another 305 were wounded. The lucky ones were greeted by large crowds gathered in Detroit and given a ticker-tape parade on July 4, 1919. Grand speeches were given, Detroit's Mayor James Couzen greeted the "Bears" by saying, "The 339th symbolizes in our minds a story of magnificent endurance, sacrifice and obedience. . . . You have made the numerals 339th the title of a long-to-be-remembered Michigan epic. . . . We pledge our utmost support in reinstating you in life."[180] Senator Johnson was invited and accepted an invitation to speak. There had been thousands of home-comings of military units since the armistice, some more, some less dramatic and eventful than that of the 339th, but never bringing with it so strong a sense that this unit was returning from the dead. Scores of times the report had come that the regiment had been wiped out. First came the rumor that the Arctic cold had engulfed them; then the Bolshevik, while outnumbering them 50 to 1, had massacred them; and even more fearful in the souls of these men came the report that they mutinied against their country. But, every time, over the thousands of miles of frozen country, over the glaciers and wastes of snow, against arctic cold, disease, hunger, and overwhelming odds, they fought and the truth came back in word that the old flag was still flying. They fought even when their officers could not tell them why they were there and what the fighting was about. Life was about to begin again for these doughboys, but memories would not be laid to rest. Memories of the friends they left behind, buried beneath Russian soil, would always be with them (See this endnote).[181] Many in the Detroit's Own Welfare Association felt the return of the soldiers was the best possible proof of the power of public opinion when once brought to bear upon the United States Government. They had organized, marched, petitioned and demanded the return of their loved ones. They believed that they played a major role in bringing them home. Local newspapers agreed:

> "Their return was the best possible proof of the power of public opinion when once brought to bear upon the military situation. You may talk as much as you like about the power of the military in time of war. But the real truth it that even the most autocratic of army authorities cannot stand up long before a public sentiment that is clearly defined, widespread, and genuinely aroused. When once American opinion had become convinced that the Polar Bears ought to be withdrawn from Northern Russia, no power on earth could keep them there, Bolsheviki or no Bolsheviki."[182]

Postscript to Chapter III:

The British evacuated Russia on September 27. They made one final push into the interior prior to evacuating, with mixed results. For the British, the summer was just as hard as the winter had been. After enduring the arctic winter conditions, the British experienced the opposite end of the spectrum with long and hot mosquito infested days. The arctic night turned into the arctic day, this time with only two hours of night.[183]

With the evacuations completed, Archangel eventually fell to the Bolsheviks on February 20, 1920. It is estimated that anywhere from five hundred to five thousand Russians were shot for cooperating with the Allies.

Other displays of the Polar Bears at the Military and Space Museum.

Picture and uniform of Cleo Colburn at the Military and Space Museum.

Stan Bozich, owner and director of Michigan's Own, Inc., Military and Space Museum, Frankenmuth, Michigan, standing in front of the museum.

THE POLAR BEARS

In the summer of 1918, President Woodrow Wilson, at the urging of Britain and France, sent an infantry regiment to north Russia to fight the Bolsheviks in hopes of persuading Russia to rejoin the war against Germany. The 339th Infantry Regiment, with the first battalion of the 310th Engineers and the 337th Ambulance and Hospital Companies, arrived at Archangel, Russia, on September 4, 1918. About 75 percent of the 5,500 Americans who made up the North Russian Expeditionary Forces were from Michigan; of those, a majority were from Detroit. The newspapers called them "Detroit's Own,"; they called themselves "Polar Bears." They marched on Belle Isle on July 4, 1919. Ninety-four of them were killed in action after the United States decided to withdraw from Russia but before Archangel's harbor thawed.

BUREAU OF HISTORY, MICHIGAN DEPARTMENT OF STATE
REGISTERED LOCAL SITE NO. 1518
PROPERTY OF THE STATE OF MICHIGAN, 1988

Historical marker at the Polar Bear Monument.

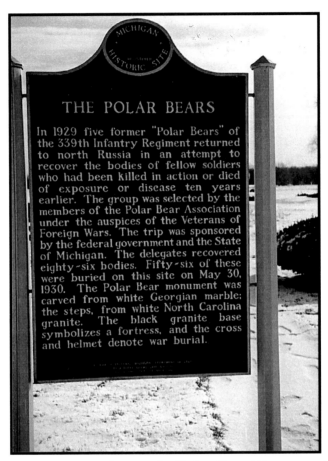

THE POLAR BEARS

In 1929 five former "Polar Bears" of the 339th Infantry Regiment returned to north Russia in an attempt to recover the bodies of fellow soldiers who had been killed in action or died of exposure or disease ten years earlier. The group was selected by the members of the Polar Bear Association under the auspices of the Veterans of Foreign Wars. The trip was sponsored by the federal government and the State of Michigan. The delegates recovered eighty-six bodies. Fifty-six of these were buried on this site on May 30, 1930. The Polar Bear monument was carved from white Georgian marble; the steps, from white North Carolina granite. The black granite base symbolizes a fortress, and the cross and helmet denote war burial.

Historical marker at the Polar Bear Monument.

Polar Bear Monument--White Chapel Memorial, Troy Michigan.

Polar Bear soldiers at attention in front of barracks at Camp Custer

Polar Bear soldiers resting at Camp Custer

CHAPTER IV

THE RED SCARE AT HOME

"Death has been swallowed up in victory." (1 Corinthians 15:54)

> If sympathy for the World's wounds is not enlarged
> by our anguish, if love for those around us is not
> expanded, if gratitude for what is good does not flame
> up, if insight is not deepened, if commitment to what
> is important is not strengthened, if aching for a new
> day is not intensified, if hope is weakened and faith
> diminished, if from the experience of death comes nothing
> good, then death has won. Then death, be proud.[184]

The war was ending – The world's warriors were beginning to feel a new breath of fresh air. Drawn from every sphere of life, from every profession, department and industry soldiers from around the world were thrust into new situations full of unknown difficulties; and behind the fighting army was the civilian army of men and women at home who gave their thoughts, their prayers, their work to the soldiers. It was time for jubilation. The people of the United States were part of the celebration. "And you will go out and leap like calves released from the stall." (Malachi 4:2) The menace that had engulfed the world for so many years was gone. The bad giant had been slain. The country could leap for joy, re-group, and begin to focus on its own problems. It was time to stop worrying about the world's affairs and concentrate on the problems at home – healing was needed. Overseas problems were "theirs" to solve, they were no longer America's problems. It was time to look within and forget the world for a while. But could that be done?

On a Friday evening in November of 1919, fifty men were gathered in Detroit to listen to a concert given by the Union of Russian Workers. It was a jovial gathering of friends who had come to relax and be entertained. The music lifted their spirits as the building echoed with beautiful melodies. Outside the building, the quiet, dark streets began to echo with engines of darkened images moving slowly toward the building from both sides. The police officers, armed with machine guns and billy-clubs, hurriedly climbed out of their vehicles, surrounded the building and awaited orders. The music penetrated the brick and mortar and floated down the again quiet street. The order was given and the police burst in from all sides. The music suddenly stopped. Many of the concert attendees had very limited understanding of English and were confused as to what was happening; they could not understand the intrusion. The police ordered them out of the building and into the large detention trucks. They were being arrested for being "red agitators." The next day newspapers declared, "Choosing the second anniversary of the Bolshevik revolution in Russia as the psychological moment to strike, the Federal Government, aided by municipal police . . . last night dealt the most serious and sweeping blow it has yet aimed at criminal anarchists."[185] The Communist Party headquarters, the House of Masses, was stripped bare and over eight hundred persons were arrested. Thirty-six persons were taken into custody in Grand Rapids and another fifty-six in Flint. Federal authorities lavishly praised Michigan law enforcement agencies for their cooperation in ending the "Red" menace in the state. The next day, an additional 250 Union of Russian Workers were arrested. Many other raids were taking place around the country. In one raid, officers forced the aliens to sing the "Star Spangled Banner."[186] The police were harsh and demanding as the people tried to explain why they were there: strictly for entertainment or just because they wanted to be there. A number of those arrested were badly beaten by the police.[187]

Attorney General A. Mitchell Palmer would later say, "If . . . some of my agents out in the field . . . were a little rough and unkind, or short and curt, with these alien agitators. . . I think it might well be over looked."[188] The year 1919 marked the beginning of the xenophobic and hysterically anti-radical Red Scare. Similar raids were being made across the country. Police were ordered to smash a few heads and ask questions later.

In Detroit, Alexander Bukowetsky was one of those arrested and later interviewed. He told of how his wife came to see him at the police station and how the police, "hit wife in the chest with a gun knocking her to the floor. . . . When I came to America I came with the thought that I was coming to a free country, a place of freedom and happiness, and I was anxious to come. . . . As much as I was anxious to come here to America, I am a hundred times more anxious to run away from Americanism."[189] For Bukowetsky and others across the country, democracy was a dream that died – a new nightmare of terror took its place.

Conditions were deplorable in Detroit. The *Nation* magazine reported that ". . . eight hundred men were imprisoned from three to six days in a dark, windowless, narrow corridor running around the big central areaway of the city's antiquated Federal building; they slept on the bare stone floor at night, in the heavy heat that welled sickeningly up to the low roof, just over their heads; they were shoved . . . by heavy-handed policemen; they were forbidden even the chance to perform even a makeshift shave; they were compelled to stand in long lines for access to the solitary drinking fountain and one toilet; they were denied all food for twenty hours, and after that they were fed on what their families brought in; and they were refused all communications with relatives or attorneys."[190]

Officials of the Justice Department admitted that they had inadvertently arrested innocent citizens, but asked the reporters not to mention that fact.[191] As examples, the raid netted a seventeen year old boy looking for a job, a number of men who stopped at the first floor café for a glass of "near-beer," and twenty-two men in a nearby building that was incorrectly identified as part of the House of Masses.

"Mankind's values, attitudes, and expectations were in disarray in 1919, and the resultant violence was worldwide."[192] Revolutionary uprisings were taking place around the world, Germany and Hungary in particular. In addition, the turmoil in Russia explained, in part, the United States government's concern for a revolution in the United States. In that same year, the American people began to see the violence first hand. During 1919, someone tried to bomb the house of Attorney General Palmer, but in so doing, blew himself up: "The act proved a godsend for those who contended that revolutionaries were tumbling off every ship."[193] Palmer, as would be expected, was badly shaken by the incident. He was convinced that the bombing was a full scale "Red" plot. It was the beginning, he thought, of a Bolshevik revolution in the United States. He began to compile lists of possible revolutionaries living in the United States including union and NAACP members. J. Edgar Hoover would later recall that, "The Communist Party USA first emerged . . . in 1919. In the beginning it seemed little more than a freak. Yet in the intervening years that freak has grown into a powerful monster endangering us all."[194]

What caused the insensitivity to civil liberties and the brutality and callousness of this period? Why was it possible that an idle remark could sentence a man to years of imprisonment? War tends to breed excesses and World War I was no exception. As usual, the villains were the outsiders: aliens, minorities and dissenters. The fear of Bolshevism was great. Could it spread to the United States? The events of 1919 that culminated in the January 1920 massive round up of suspected "Reds," would seem to answer that question in the affirmative. Fear had grabbed hold of the American dream to work hard and enjoy the fruits of one's labor. It seemed to many Americans that this dream was about to be taken away by strangers from other lands, the newspapers called them Bolsheviks. Terrible reports were emerging from other countries about this new menace that was invading their lands. Front page headlines read, "Lenine Exploits China And India," and "Murders Around The World."[195] It seemed to the American public, an epidemic of vast proportions had somehow escaped its borders and now threatened the entire world.

When World War I ended on November 11, 1918, America had close to 1,500 political prisoners either in jail or awaiting trial, according to the National Civil Liberties Bureau. Persecution for unpopular ideas did not decrease when the war ended. During the war the government thought it essential to have conformity and be intolerant of anything that resembled anti-Americanism.

When American soldiers returned from Europe, they began to tell stories without the cover of government censorship. They were upset at the European Allies and felt betrayed and bitter toward them. Mostly, these vented feelings came out of frustration with the war itself. However, the stories told by the veterans began to turn public opinion against foreign entanglements and particularly foreigners living in the United States. Also, the returning veterans were faced with unemployment lines. During the four years of the war, America had become rich with war orders. Now, many businesses had to close. Nine million Americans were put out of work; in addition, another four million veterans were looking for jobs (15,000 veterans were being discharged daily).[196] With few controls, industries either closed or began the task of retooling. On top of it all, the cost of living doubled between 1914 and 1919 as inflation soared. Detroit was no exception: "Detroit, which had seen sharp rises in employment and inflation during the war years, now suffered sharp depression. Many small businesses failed during the postwar slump. Merciless layoffs occurred at the larger ones."[197]

The depression was more effective than Attorney General Palmer in combating the unions. The majority of the 175,000 Detroit auto workers and thousands in other industries were thrown out of work. Detroit teachers were also warned not to join the newly formed American Federation of Teachers, or risk losing their renewal contracts. They were thankful for a job, but they were not happy at making $200.00 a year less than janitors.[198]

Between 1870 and 1930 Detroit had a tremendous increase in immigrants. They came from almost every corner of the world. So numerous were they that in 1900 twelve per cent of the population of Detroit spoke no English. No other major city could make that claim.[199]

The first ethnic groups to arrive in mass, other than the British and Canadian, who moved to Detroit and other parts of the country were the Germans and Irish. They endeavored to preserve their homelands' heritage by continuing their cultures and languages. Eventually, streaming into Detroit were the Poles, Italians, Greeks, Arabs, Russians, Slovaks, Romanians, Swedes, Finns, and many others. They formed pockets of sanctuaries that allowed them to speak and carry on everyday activities as if they were still in their homelands. Their way of life was seen by some Americans, however, as contempt for American culture. This cultural dynamic was happening all across the land. Many of the union leaders spoke with German-Jewish and Russian-Jewish accents. "Jews had, in fact, fathered both the German and the Russian labor movements. In Russia the repression's of the czarist government had radicalized the labor movement. Many of its leaders were Communists. When the Communists in March, 1919, founded the Third International to ferment world revolution, many Americans began to associate the Russian-accented labor leaders in the United States with the . . . revolutionaries in Russia."[200]

Unemployment, inflation, and bitterness toward foreigners made Detroit and America, in 1919, a place of seething tensions. While the war was fought, whatever was wrong with America was blamed on Germany or the radicals at home. When the war ended, who would be blamed for the problems? The American public looked and saw the answer – Bolshevism. "The Red Scare was an extension of the atmosphere of the war, with its cult of patriotism, its generalized climate of violence, and its need of an enemy."[201]

Families across America learned in 1917, that a group of people in Russia called the Bolsheviks had seized power and had killed the Czar and his family. Civil war in that country had erupted. The public was also told that Lenin not only called for the workers in Russia to unite, but also spoke to the workers of the world to unite and overthrow the ruling classes. This was a frightening message to many countries including the United States. As the war came to a close, the harsh feelings against Germany turned into an anti-Bolshevik crusade. They were now the new American scapegoat. The American government felt it essential to keep American boys fighting in Russia to eliminate the source of this menace. If the government felt it necessary to fight in Russia, it must be a major concern for all Americans, at least that is what the public was reading. Editorials were quoting speeches made at socialist gatherings that inflamed the American public:

> This country had incorrect news regarding affairs in Russia.
> I do not want American soldiers and the American Republic
> to put down a growing republic about 6,000 miles away who
> are struggling for freedom," he said, "While Russia apparently
> grows freer, the United States. . ." Here he stopped and smiled,
> causing the assemblage to laugh and applaud heartily.[202]

Other editorials proclaimed the righteousness of staying in Russia to eliminate all remnant of this cancer but questioned why we were not sending more to the fight. Also note the naiveté of the time as the President is canonized in his decision making:

> Senator Hitchcock sufficiently explained to the Senate why we had sent troops to Russia, but he was not so fortunate in explaining why we had sent so few. He said that the Administration had been criticized first for not yielding to the desire of Britain and France that a large force of troops be sent there, and then for sending any at all: and this, he said illustrated "the embarrassment that confronted President Wilson in deciding what policy to adopt." Surely this does not properly represent the Administration. Confronted by two opposite criticisms, the President cannot have decided to compromise by trying to please both by sending troops, but not troops enough. This is what Mr. Hitchcock implies, and he cannot be correct. The only question before the President was what would be right and necessary, not what would please two irreconcilable sets of critics.[203]

Another editorial in the same paper proclaimed that it was "unworthy" to say the Bolsheviks were an acceptable form of humanity.

Other articles explained why the United States needed to continue the fight: "It is the duty of the allied policy to help in these hard times the honest Russian people, groaning under the yoke of the Bolsheviki, but not to betray them and the small number of intelligent Russians, delivering them into the hands of arbitrary ruffians."[204]

American newspapers asked the question; what about the ruffians in the United States? If Trotsky had sailed from New York to help launch the Revolution in Russia, whom had he left behind?

The media also brought out the "big guns" for this fight. Pages of quotations from historian George Kennan filled newspaper sheets across the country. He vehemently defended the duty of the United States to fight and defeat the Bolsheviks in Russia.[205] The "Grandmother of the Russian Revolution" was proclaimed to be Mme. Breshkovskaya. She was sailing from Russia to the United States in 1919 and granted an interview to a Seattle newsman. She was reported to say that the "Bolshviki's are destroyers." She wanted a revolution against the terrible human conditions in Russia, but considered her homeland under Bolshevism as no better off than under the Czar.[206] Even the Ambassador to Russia, David R. Francis, urged the American Government not to withdraw troops. He wanted the fighting continued against an evil that could destroy the entire world.[207]

Because the war was not officially over until the summer of 1920 when the treaties were finally signed, the American government continued to be hostile toward radicals in 1919. They continued to use the Espionage and Sedition Acts that were used during wartime and the Immigration Act of 1903: saying the wrong thing could cause imprisonment. These acts gave the government the power to arrest and deport citizens of any country with which America was at war, or to expel any alien considered to be dangerous. There need not be a reason given to put a person in jail, during this time, and the alien had little or no defense. Any immigrant who believed in or belonged to any organization that espoused violence could be deported. Even the Postmaster General continued to ban publications he believed were anti-American. For the first time in American history, immigrants were jailed for espousing certain beliefs even if they did not act upon them.

An editorial in the *Syracuse Post-Standard* proclaimed, "Whenever there is trouble of any sort in America there are voices shouting, 'Bolshevism.'"[208] Because the year 1919 had so many troubling problems for the United States, the public believed it was caused by some outside influence. This influence, people surmised, was being transported into the country by foreigners arriving in the United States.

It was easy to blame all the country's ills on these strangers landing on America's shores.

The year 1919 started with an ominous tone when in January 35,000 shipyard workers in Seattle, Washington, went on strike for higher wages and shorter hours. Other labor leaders in Seattle called a general strike to support the strikers' cause. An additional 60,000 workers went on strike in February. Seattle was nearly paralyzed. To many Americans around the country, the strike was the beginning of the Bolshevik revolution in this country. The newspaper writers began to realize that Red Scare articles sold as well as German scare stories. One Seattle paper declared, "Reds Directing Seattle Strike To Test Chance For Revolution."[209] The Seattle mayor picked up on the hysteria and announced, "The anarchists in this community shall not rule its affairs..." and then asked for federal troops. The strikers wanted better pay, not a fight on Bolshevism, and eventually called off the strike. The mayor remarked that the rebellion had been quelled. The *New York Times* carried his enthusiastic words with the headline banner, "Anarchists Tried Revolution In Seattle, But Never Got To First Base, Says Mayor Hanson."

There were three other major strikes in 1919, and each time the unions were categorized as Bolshevik sympathizers. The first was in September when the Boston police department went on strike. The strikers were immediately labeled as Bolsheviks and were fired.

The same month, almost 400,000 steel workers struck in Philadelphia. Many of the strikers wanted better pay and working conditions. The average pay was $28.00 a week for seven twelve hour days. The steel executives called the strike "un-American." *The Wall Street Journal* announced the steel companies were "fighting the battle of the American Constitution."[210]

Riots took place as the police and private guards tried to break the picket lines. Shots were fired and men on both sides were killed and injured. The American public, fueled by the media, blamed it on the Bolsheviks. The strikers had no choice but to go back to work with nothing gained.

Just as the steel strike was ending, the coal miners walked off their jobs across the country. Their leader, John L. Lewis expressed strong anti-Bolshevik comments, but the mine owners knew what was needed to stop the strike. The owners announced that the strike was ordered by none other than Lenin himself![211] A court order was easily obtained to stop the strike.

Newspaper stories in February and March brought the Bolshevik threat vividly into the homes of the American family. Bolshevism was the dreaded disease that had no cure. The news media seemed to think that the country needed to be immunized by painful injections of information. Each newspaper publisher was the willing doctor. Headlines filled each day's paper with "'Red Book' Discovered At Headquarters Of Union," "Says Army Courts bred Bolsheviks," and "Senator Warns Of Impending Danger If Discharged Soldiers Are Not Employed."[212] Each day writers employed new and alarming headlines. Editorials that not only branded the "Bolsheviks as less socialists and more of an organized bunch of misguided thieves,"[213] but also called upon the President to send more troops to Russia. One such editor quoted the Chairman of the Executive Committee of the American-Russian Chamber of Commerce as saying, "If the Allies did not interfere in Russia and establish order, the country would sink to such complete anarchy that a German would be able to step in as dictator and organize it on a German basis."[214] This was scary verbiage to the American people – using the two dreaded words of the day, Bolsheviks and Germans.

Americans were reading stories about how some U.S. workers such as Detroit Ford Works employee, Herbert Spencer Calvert, gave technical aid to help the new Soviet state in the operation of blast furnaces and other machine processes for the newly developing steel industry.[215] Even the YMCA, which started in Detroit, seemed to be challenging the"American way." The newspapers proclaimed that the Executive Director, Sherwood Eddy, after a visit to Russia felt that the Soviet Union was "a challenge to the rest of the world, to nations ruled by swollen, selfish capitalism."[216]

Throughout March, articles were appearing in newspapers and magazines demanding further U.S. intervention:[217] "The Russian question is vital, as it is necessary in the interest of peace to bar the westward route of Bolshevism. . . . Peace was impossible while Europe [and the United States] was threatened by a Bolshevist army in which there were many German officers."[218] The loud cry of outrage was drowning out the still small voices that were barely noticeable– those like Senator Johnson of California, and the Michigan families wanting their sons back.

Opposition to the intervention was at first geographical. Senator Lawrence Y. Sherman of Illinois spoke out against the American presence in Russia on February 14. His analogy between the German attack on Belgium and the Allied intervention was interesting, as it struck a raw nerve in Congress by comparing the "Hun's" actions to that of the United States:

> There is no escaping the verdict of history. We may declaim for months; we may issue proclamations by the score; communiqués from the peace conference; stately phrases may emanate from the absent Executive; but history, with unerring verdict and with impartial pen, will write the record for the future years. If we remain in Russia under present conditions, without a new government being set up there, with all the characteristics that belong to civil government, and we do not recognize such a government, and enter

or remain there by its consent, we have no business in northern Russia under the rule of international right. We can justify it only by brute force; by the law of necessity, that admits there is no other law, we can invoke our defense. So there is a distinction ever to be kept in mind. I do not say, save by the law of necessity, that we are rightfully, or ever were rightfully, in northern Russia. We went there with our Allies by the extengencies [sic] of war for the purpose of preventing the Bolshevist government from either submitting or voluntarily consenting to the establishment of a submarine base in the neighborhood of Archangel and to protect our Allies' military supplies; it would have been a military loss. So forces were dispatchedthere to protect them. Those are two good military reasons, but they savor too much of the Hun.

On March 3, Senator Porter J. McCumber of North Dakota introduced several letters from American citizens supporting further action in Russia. One such letter crystallized the problem succinctly: "While we are debating the subject of restricting the menace of this accursed creed in America, few seem to realize the necessity of crushing it in the place of its inception." Another letter read in part: "There is something humiliating and unaccountable in the frantic haste of our Congress to hurry our troops back home, regardless of our responsibilities to the world.[219] It was a two edged sword. Could the United States successfully defeat the Bolsheviks at home without eliminating the source? That was the question many people were asking.

In New York City, the police arrested 200 suspected Bolsheviks and "found radical leaflets." The police were reported as saying, "Many were anarchist and admitted it." The newspaper's report said that these "workmen closely banded together and solemnly pledged to the destruction of all governments. . . . This [Red] book binds members of the Soviet forcibly to take possession of all . . . through violence of social revolution and to accomplish the overthrow and destruction of all institutions of government and ownership."[220]

The American public reeled in horror – the American way of life was about to be eradicated by this treacherous virus. Who would be the next victim? What person or city would be next to fall? As a frightened America held its collective breath, the expected happened.

On April 28, 1919, a homemade bomb was delivered to the office of Mayor Hanson of Seattle. The next day a similar bomb was delivered to the home of a former Georgia Senator. The Seattle bomb did not detonate, but the maid of the Senator opened the package and was severely injured. Hanson declared the acts were not labor disputes but ones of revolutionary anarchy.[221] His words were quoted in Seattle headlines and picked up by other newspapers that were eager for more Bolshevik news: "Says All Cities Must Clear Out The I.W.W. And Bolsheviki."[222]

Thirty-four more bombs were sent through the mail in the next few days.[223] Judges, senators, businessmen, and cabinet members were all singled out. All the bombs were mailed just before May Day, seemingly to arrive on May 1 (Traditionally celebrated as a spring festival and, in recent times, celebrated in some countries by demonstrations commemorating labor). No one was ever arrested for these bombs, but the media continued to pursue the Bolshevik theory. The anger of the American people continued to rise.[224] The political arrests continued. In Boston, "radicals' were picked up including the "youngest man to get Harvard Degree."[225] It was now obvious to Americans that the Bolsheviks were in the schools too. A New York editorial read:

> 'Down with everybody who wears a collar or a clean shirt.' That is the pemmican of Bolshevism. It is not only meat for strong men, it is milk for babes. Our high school boys are to be fed on it. The teacher of English at the Commercial High School finds his pupils reading "The Bolsheviks and the Soviets," a pamphlet by that industrious propagandist of Bolshevism in the United States, Mr. Albert R. Williams, and ' A Letter to the American Workingman,'

ascribed to the master sculptor of Russian ruin, Nikolai Lenine. If our youth are to learn the science of destruction at school; if, instead of filling the too brief time of their education with study of free representative government, of the democratic polity under which they live, they are to be indoctrinated in theories of class intolerance and supremacy put into bloody practice before their eyes in Russia; if the intolerable horror and shame that have brought a mighty nation to despair are to be the model and example of our future citizens, we had better close the schools or turn them into penitentiaries for the assassins they will breed.[226]

Not only did many believe they were in the school system, but the front page of the *New York Times* proclaimed the Bolsheviks would soon be dictating when Americans could marry! They reported that all Bolshevik girls must be married by age 18 and the boys at age 21.[227]

The May 7 newspaper brought shocking news to the reader: "Hints of a Bolshiviki plan to hold up New York City in some unexplained way for an hour, as a spectacular demonstration to the world that the 'red' brotherhood had developed fighting strength on this city. . . ."[228] The largest city in the United States was to be put on hold for one hour by this spreading menace. The threat never happened.

Just after 11 p.m. on June 2, 1919, a bomb exploded in the entrance of United States Attorney General A. Mitchell Palmer's home. Similar attacks occurred in eight other cities.[229] The explosions caused extensive property damage and two deaths. Many Americans surmised who the culprits were even before arrests were made.[230] The newspapers declared, "Palmer and Family Safe - Red literature Found."[231] The public was demanding action – how did these anarchist get into the country? The answer must lie, they reasoned, in the immigration procedures. The newspapers reported Senator King's thoughts: "Removal from office of Frederic C. Howe, Commissioner of Immigrants at Ellis Island has been demanded by Senator

King of Utah. . . . There should be no official there who would be willing to give Bolshviki coming from Europe the glad hand."[232]

The American people were fed-up with what they perceived as outside influences that interfered with the American way of life. The saying, "100% Americanism" became popular in 1919 as a way to protest against anyone or anything that was not American. Unions, liberals, blacks, Catholics, Jews and aliens were suspect. The "100% Americanism" permeated the mind and soul of the country. Schools, newspapers, churches and businesses were told to look for Bolsheviks among their people. The epithet "Bolshevism" was used effectively in damning any beliefs that were contrary to the "American way."

The American Legion was founded in 1919 by veterans of the first World War. Their first and foremost theme was "100% Americanism." They became the muscle to rid the country of this plague. Their slogan was, "Leave the Reds to the Legion." The Legion lived up to their slogan, as they used their muscle to stop marches, and were possibly involved in killing a suspected Bolshevik leader in Centralia, Washington. No one was ever arrested for the killing. The coroner's report said, ". . . (he) broke out of jail, went to the . . . bridge, and committed suicide. He jumped off with a rope around his neck and then shot himself full of holes."

Congress formed a committee, headed by Senator Lee Overman, to investigate the Bolshevik threat, if any. The Overman Committee, without showing any evidence, declared that a possible revolution was about to break loose in the country. They declared that Bolshevism must be stopped.[233]

Clayton R. Lusk, a New York state legislator, also investigated the Bolshevik threat and authorized a series of raids on radical and immigrant organizations. He even proposed a loyalty oath requirement for all school teachers.

Other states were also beginning to act. Thirty-two states outlawed the red flag. From 1919 to 1920, over 1,400 people were arrested for violating sedition or red flag legislation.[234]

On July 4, in Detroit, a report by Samuel Gompers, President of the American Federation of Labor, was made to Washington on the "Conditions in the State of Michigan." His statement, submitted to the Judiciary Committee, "makes the charge that the prohibition forces are aiding and abetting Bolshevism by oppressive legislation depriving the workers of their beer." He reasoned that it was "breeding class hatred on an alarming scale."[235] Bolshevism had become the culprit of all the evils in the world, even the lack of beer!

The *New York Times*, on July 5, wrote a scathing editorial on Bolshevism in Michigan:

> Michigan use to be regarded as one of the most conservative States in the Union. So far as the industrial part of her population is concerned, she must be one of the most radical, to judge by accumulating evidence. No one can call the Socialist Party conservative, and yet it was obliged recently to expel the entire Michigan branch for going over to Bolshevism. It is true that the Michigan men do not call themselves Bolsheviki, but they are certainly in full sympathy with (them). . . . Michigan has received, within the last few years, an extraordinarily large increase in its laboring population, due to the increase in many of its industries, and a great number of the newcomers are foreigner. It is no longer the same State that it was ten years ago.[236]

The editorial was correct; Michigan was not the same state it had been in the past. The state was witnessing an influx of many foreigners earnestly looking for work to feed their families. Foreigners were looked upon with suspicion, and Michigan had its full share of newcomers. But Michigan was also being torn from within by the pain it still felt for the returning soldiers. It was a time of joy and celebration but also a time to weep over the spilled blood of so many Michigan boys.

These soldiers had fought for seven months after the war had ended and many arrived home in boxes. The soul of the state was wrenched not only by so many new faces speaking unknown languages, but also by the desperate, disparaging feeling that no one had cared that its boys had died in a far away, God-forsaken land.

While the country strived to fight the evil called Bolshevism here at home, Michigan was called upon to fight this evil at home and abroad; it was not sure it deserved that privilege. Michigan was grieving with bitterness; the newspapers had demanded for months the return of their boys from Russia, but in most other states, newspapers quoted officials such as Senator Swanson of the Foreign Relations Committee: "It would be cowardly for us to withdraw now."[237]

Millions in America saw the red completely engulfing the white and blue. Any strikes were part of the plot; Blacks and Catholics were part of the plot; college professors were part of the plot; Wall Street and foreigners were part of the plot. Fear of a complete Bolshevik take-over of the United States was everywhere.

Dr. W. E. B. DuBois, founder of the National Association for the Advancement of Colored People (NAACP), was quoted in the May, 1919 issue of *The Crisis*. He stated that the Bolshevik Revolution was "the one new idea of the World War – the idea which may well stand in future years as the one thing that made the slaughter worthwhile."

Attorney General Palmer had political aspirations that could profit from a plan to eliminate the Bolshevik plot. The elections of 1920 would bring a new president. The man who could successfully destroy the "Red" threat might easily be swept into the White House. Palmer decided to establish an anti-radical division within the Bureau of Investigation. With much fan-fare, Palmer put in charge of the division the twenty-four year old J. Edgar Hoover. Hoover would begin to make lists of suspected radicals (his count was over 60,000), with an emphasis on aliens. "The history of the Communist Party in the United States," Hoover would later say, "is characterized by two main trends: (1) The development of a disciplined Party structure or in the words of William Z. Foster, 'the building of a Leninist Party of a new type,' and (2) the complete and unquestioning subservience of the Party to Soviet Russia."[238] Hoover promised to fight this menace.

with all necessary means. In October of 1919 President Wilson suffered a stroke. Very little direction would come from the White House for the next seventeen months, especially on the Bolshevik threat. This allowed Palmer and Hoover a freer hand to direct and implement the eradication of this perceived threat.

November 7 and 8 brought about what many Americans had been demanding: the arrest in mass of the troublemakers. Raids were conducted across the country on the Union of Russian Workers. One weekend netted hundreds of aliens, and "tons of seditious literature." The newspapers also reported, "Palmer To Deport Reds."[239] J. Edgar Hoover obtained the use of an army transport ship called the Buford that hastened the deportation process. The aliens were escorted to the ship, which the media coined the "Soviet Ark," on December 21. Bitterness toward these aliens seemed to permeate the American people even in the church pulpits. The famous preacher Billy Sunday declared, "I would stand them up before a firing squad, and save space on our ships."[240]

Deportation was not a criminal procedure. It involved neither judge nor jury. An unwanted alien was given a hearing before an immigration official. Thus, even after an appeal, he could be deported.

More bombs exploded in December that destroyed the homes of Justice Robert Van Moschataker of the Pennsylvania Supreme Court; William B. Mills, acting Superintendent of Philadelphia's Police Department; and Ernest T. Trigg, President of Philadelphia's Chamber of Commerce. Everyone demanded action.

Hoover and Palmer decided for a clean sweep of the terrorist. They planned January 2, 1920, as the day for arresting as many radicals as possible across the country. The main purpose of the raids was to arrest aliens. If United States citizens were found at the meeting they were to be turned over to the local authorities. The agents were ordered to establish the fact that the persons arrested were members of the Communist Party of America or the Communist Labor Party. Membership in either group was ground enough for deportation. Over 3,000 warrants for the arrest of aliens were signed. January 2, 1920, would become a night of terror for many families. In a series of dramatic raids, more than 4,000 people were arrested in 33 cities. So many people were being arrested that one newspaper called for the construction of concentration camps to house these and future detainees.[241]

Detroit was one of the biggest targets; over 1,000 men and boys were rounded up in raids throughout the city and placed in a federal building while waiting for a hearing. They had to step over each other to move about, and slept on the stone floor at night. There was one water fountain and one toilet for all the prisoners. For the first 20 hours they were not fed; then, they were given one cup of coffee and two biscuits twice a day. Some of the wives of the prisoners were not told the whereabouts of their husbands for up to six days.[242]

By the end of the sixth day of incarceration, 350 prisoners had been released for lack of evidence. About 140 of those still under arrest were transferred to another building. On the way to the new site, newspaper photographers took pictures of the unshaven, unkempt men. The American people were shown the pictures and agreed that these prisoners matched their own vision of a Bolshevik. The *Washington Post* wrote, "There is no time to waste in hair-splitting over infringement of liberty." However, Detroit's mayor, James Couzen, protested vehemently against the entire action.[243] His voice of reason was not heard however, because fear was louder and carried a bigger club. Mayor Couzens labored to maintain a rational atmosphere. He finally demanded that the prisoners receive humane treatment and that the Detroit police should no longer cooperate with federal authorities. The general public, however, praised Palmer and urged him to continue his crusade. Editorials continued to fan the flames:

> If some or any of us, impatient for the swift confusion of the Reds, have ever questioned the alacrity, resolute will, and fruitful, intelligent vigor of the Department of Justice in hunting down those enemies of the United States, the questioners and the doubters have now cause to approve and applaud. The agents of the department have planned with shrewdness and a large wisdom, and carried out with extraordinary success, the nabbing of nearly four thousand radicals, Communists and Communist Laborites, differentiated by name only, all working for the destruction of the Government of the United States, and the establishing in its place the Soviet State that has brought so much happiness and prosperity to Russia. . . . These energuments of proletarian autocracy and the knocking in the head of the 'bourgeoisie' – which Americans are – have been gathered from many towns and cities. All over the country these devisors of social and economic ruin were found; and this 'raid' is only a beginning.

Even the defeated Germans were implicated in Bolshevik action across the country. *The Cleveland News* ran headlines that connected the two: "German Hand In U.S. Red Plots." The paper went on to say, "Germans, if not Germany, are among the ringleaders of the 'reds' movement in the United States and the Allied countries. Proof of this is in the hands of the Department of Justice here." No evidence was ever produced. Another article in the same paper blamed the increased cost of living on the "reds": "Federal Agents Free To Act After Red Roundup To Start Drive On Excessive Prices."[244]

The years 1919 to 1920 brought very little proof of a Communist conspiracy to start a revolution in the United States. There were, however, Communist organizations that existed, but their numbers were small. One such organization began in Michigan: "In May, 1920, a 'unity' convention of the Communist Labor Party and a faction . . . of the Communist party was secretly held at Bridgman, Michigan, resulting in the formation of the United Communist Party of America.[245]

The Palmer raids and the action of many state legislatures marked the peak of the Red Scare. Americans began to realize that perhaps Palmer and many others had over-reacted – civil rights of innocent people had been violated. The Palmer raids helped shock Americans into realizing that the Bill of Rights was meant for all people, not only citizens.

With little regard for due process, the United States government from 1919 to 1920 arrested thousands of suspected radicals. In these illegal raids, born of national hysteria, those arrested often were roughed up, denied access to lawyers, and sometimes not fed properly. Most of the warrants were later thrown out of court, and Congress drew back in horror over the creature it had unleashed.

It is also interesting to note what the words, "Red Scare" meant to Michigan, compared to the rest of the country. To Michigan, those words cut straight to the fear in one's soul; it was the gut-wrenching evil overseas that kept their men from coming home – the giant in an unknown land that devoured peaceable people and left its own country in ruin. Why was it Michigan's responsibility, they would ask, to stop this march of evil? Oh, to be true, reports of Bolshevik raids and men being arrested around the country and in Detroit were reported, but the eyes of the state were looking abroad. The words "Red Scare" evoked unending questions that never seemed to get answered: Why was the government committing such a small force to fight the Bolsheviks? Why were the soldiers treated so poorly by their own Allies? Why were they forgotten by their own government? Why were they even fighting in Russia? Those two words caused a bewildering array of nauseating feelings that only time would settle.

To the United States in general, the Red Scare was a battle within. The pulse of the rest of the nation was centered on watching and arresting Bolsheviks living behind them and next door. The nation carried very few news articles of the operations overseas, and then, only to quote "experts" on the reasons for continuing the fight.

Although subversion and sabotage, such as the bombings of government officials' residences, dotted the landscape during 1919, critics of the radicals blamed every sort of disorder on them. The "search for the inner enemy," as the sociologist George Simmel observed, "became institutionalized after World War I and then instead of being disapproved by members of one's group for being prejudiced, one was punished for not being prejudiced."

Blame was important to administer because the American public needed to feel the reassurance that the Republic's foundation was safe and secure – that it was only an outside agitation that was causing all of the problems. Americans could face an enemy, as they did the Germans, and defeat them.

It was easier to pick an enemy than to wrestle with the complex theme that the country was maturing and experiencing the growth pains of a nation. Americans looked around and picked an adversary to fight. It would be a fight that would last for the next seventy years. The cancer overseas had spread to our shores, and it had to be contained with or without the Bill of Rights.

CHAPTER V

A SAD AND TRAGIC ENDING

... Mr. Wilson ... should be judged by what he was and did prior to August 4th, 1918, the date of the papers justifying the attack on Russia. That was the first of his acts which was unlike him; and I am sure the beginning of the sad end.

> – Justice Louis D. Brandeis, May 11, 1924, to the President of the University of Virginia, Edwin A. Alderman

After the war was over, Woodrow Wilson spent the remaining days of his life trying to convince Congress and the people of the United States that the League of Nations was an important by-product of the war. He had put the troubles in Russia aside, the urgent need was for a world organization to prevent future wars. Author E. M. Halliday suggests that, "It would seem that the aftermath of the Bolshevik revolution had proved so distressing and baffling to Wilson that now he preferred almost to ignore it, or to pretend it did not exist, than to face up to the hard realities it imposed on American and Allied foreign policy." Historian George Kennan, surmised "that what was in Wilson's mind, when he avoided reference to the struggle with the Bolsheviks, was the fond hope that the mere arrival of American ... forces in Russia might touch off a 'spontaneous, democratic action.'" Halliday concludes this thought by saying, "In all of modern history there may never have been a fonder hope, more thoroughly doomed to disappointment."[246] The intervention in Russia had ended, but questions continued to be asked about the motives of the intervening powers. The Allied presence in Russia in 1919 would also color future relations between the United States and Russia. "But in the annals of the cold war the Soviet-

American combat of 1918-1919 has not lost its significance. It was a painful beginning, and clearly it must be weighted in any realistic analysis. . . between America and the U.S.S.R. 'We remember,' said Nikita Khrushchev in Los Angeles in September, 1959, 'the grim days when American soldiers went to our soil headed by their generals to help our White Guard combat the new revolution. . . . Never have any of our soldiers been on American soil, but your soldiers were on Russian soil.'"[247]

President Wilson was unaware that American soldiers were used in the fight against Russian forces.[248] It was his intent that the Americans be sent to guard storage deposes and nothing further. Kennan noted that, "The wording of the *aide-memoire* of July 17 made plain only one thing: the United States did not believe in or agree with the British plans for penetration into the Russian interior . . . and was not prepared to see American forces used." He then criticized the American officials by saying that, "At no time did any responsible American official, knowing the President's mind. . . attempt to talk out with responsible British officials the differences here involved. . . . No forewarning was given to the British of the President's decision; they had, accordingly, no opportunity to comment on it, to raise questions about it. . . . They were to have full command . . . over the American forces involved; but they had no voice in defining the purpose to which the forces in question were to be put."[249] Was Wilson so naive to believe that he need only make this request and it would be carried out? Yes, so it seems, he did believe things would flow automatically, without further attention on his part.

The British decided to use the force given to them as they pleased with some disdain: "One gains the impression that the Americans were regarded by many of the British. . . not as partners with whom a real and intimate understanding was to be sought, but rather as stupid children."[250] These children could be forced to do whatever the British wanted without regard for their understanding of the situation.

The British idea was to take full advantage of the situation until the American government demanded a change; the demand never came. Wilson also believed that the mere presence of the Allied forces would generate a peasant up-rising that would topple the Bolsheviks, another belief that did not materialize.[251]

Several people involved with the situation eventually wrote about the experience. General John J. Pershing wrote, "I was opposed to the idea [the intervention] as it would simply mean scattering our resources. . . . But the President was prevailed upon to help and I was directed to send a regiment." He later recalled that our purpose was "to guard stores and make it safe for Russian forces to come together in the north. . . . also . . . that solemn assurance by the governments united for action should be given the people of Russia that no interference with her political sovereignty or intervention in internal affairs or impairment of territorial integrity was intended."[252] Since the American forces stayed in Russia several months after the War's truce and involved themselves in military action against the Bolshevik government, the "no interference" comment is ludicrous, at best. General William S. Graves would later write: "I doubt if any unbiased person would ever hold that the United States did not interfere in the internal affairs of Russia. By this interference, the United States helped to bolster up, by its military forces, a monarchistically inclined and unpopular Government, of which the great mass of the people did not approve."[253] He also insisted that his superiors wanted him to fight Bolsheviks, "rather than as ordered [to guard] by the Secretary of War."[254]

Another officer wrote in his diary, "When the last battalion set sail from Archangel, not a soldier knew, no, not even vaguely, why he had fought or why his comrades were left behind – so many of them beneath the wooden crosses."[255] E. M. Halliday agreed when he wrote, "Few campaigns have ever been fought by American soldiers in greater ignorance of what they were about."[256] Historian Richard Pipes believed the initial engagement was clear, it was later that the motives were questioned: "Until the November 1918 Armistice, the objective of Allied intervention in Russia had been clear: to reactivate the Eastern front by helping Russians prepare to continue the war against Germany. After November 11, its purpose turned murky."[257]

A letter written by the Secretary of War, Newton D. Baker, confirmed that the campaign of North Russia was a failure and a mistake. He stated that it was not a good move militarily but was done for the cooperation of the Allies only. Mr. Baker told of how the Allies were informed that the newly established North Russian Republic had vast armies awaiting reorganization to swing to the side of the Allies. After studying the situation, he wrote to General Tasker Bliss:

> None of us can see the military value of the proposal and we assume that other considerations moved in favor of it. . . . It seems to me that our Allies want the United States to commit itself to expeditions to various places where after the war they alone will have. . . special interests. We must fight somewhere, and we originally selected France, at the request of the Allies themselves.[258]

He would later say that, "Nothing can now be gained by harsh criticism of a great President, now dead, for his ill-advised act." He also conjectured that it was surprising that "the little handful was not massacred. . . although a conjecture is that Bolshevik political shrewdness judged better than to annihilate the Allies force entirely."[259] General Bliss replied to Baker's letter that because of the huge track of land involved, it would require a large contingent to control all the needed railroads and communication lines.

Lloyd George agreed with the President that the Czarst government was as equally disagreeable as the Bolshevik regime. He also wrote that the Allies had incorrectly assumed that the Russians citizens would join an anti-Bolshevik crusade. George continued by saying:

> This easy interference overlooked his hostility to the old order, that kept him and his family in toiling in squalid wretchedness throughout their lives to uphold the extravagant profligate and corrupt aristocracy and bureaucracy which had brought disaster upon Holy Russia. Choosing between the two evils, the peasant preferred the one that put an end to his misery and bondage of centuries. Like the French peasants, who were not Jacobins, but were eager to get free from the servitude and to have free soil, that is why they supported the revolution.[260]

Confessing that the entire Allied operation was a "miserable failure," and the planned peasant uprising was a tactical blunder, he felt, however, it was not honorable to leave the Russian people in the hands of a ruthless government. It was a moral obligation for the Allies to stay and assist them in their internal struggle:

> To withdraw support from them the moment they had ceased to be useful to us and leave them to the mercy of their relentless foes without giving them a chance to save themselves or to make terms, would have been an act of dishonor.[261]

Lloyd George's comments are honorable, but how practical? The question must have been asked by others on the scene; how could a small band of Allied soldiers prevent the inevitable? This honor bound man was committing American soldiers to their death.

Winston Churchill had much to say about the intervention. He was the voice that called for the elimination of "this evil" in the world: "The day will come when it will be recognized without a doubt throughout the civilized world that the strangling of Bolshevism at birth would have been an untold blessing to the human race."[262] History may have proven him prophetic. The prominent Russian historian

Dmitri Volkogonov commented in his latest book, *Lenin,* after studying thousand of once secret files, that Lenin was "evil" personified. Volkognov's findings asserted that Lenin unquestionably initiated the terror that his successor, Josef Stalin, used to kill millions. To achieve the Communist Utopia, Lenin would not stop at anything, including terrorism, lies, hostage-taking, and the destruction of more than 70,000 churches.[263] Other secret documents also were reported by Geli Ryabov of the *Moscow News* that refuted a seventy year old account of the killing of Czar Nicholas II and his family. It had generally been accepted that the Red Army panicked and killed the family when the White Army approached. Ryabov reported he had uncovered evidence that Lenin, himself, ordered the killings.[264] Churchill understood, according to Richard Pipes, that Leninism's dominating principle was unappeasable conflict with all non-Communist countries.[265] Pipes also agreed with Churchill's assessment that a strong show of force by the Allies would have scattered the Bolshevik force and enabled the White Russian Army to advance quickly throughout the country side. Commentator Robert Conquest recounted, "As to the real Allied military effort, when it was wrongly reported that two British divisions had landed at Murmansk, Lev Karakhan, a leading Bolshevik, told the British official Bruce Lockhart. . . the Party would go underground. Certainly quite a small force could have determined the outcome."[266] Churchill was upset with the half- hearted effort his own country showed in this commitment, when the outcome was so obvious to him; but even more so at the Americans for giving even less.

American Ambassador to Russia, David R. Francis, insisted the intervention failed, not from any lack of Russian internal support, but simply from a lack of resolve on the Allies' part. A complete commitment by the United States was necessary to help the Russian people, he insisted. He also thought it was the moral obligation of the United States to help because we owed the Russian people much:

She is the chief victim of the war. Her industries have been wrecked; her transportation lines are idle for want of motive power and equipment; her intelligentsia are in exile; her capital is deserted and infested with epidemics and racked by famine. She defended the Union when England was close to recognizing the Confederacy and during the Panic of 1893, Russia tendered 300 million dollars in gold, although we refused the offer, good will was present. Lest we forget that Russia sold our Government Alaska for seven million dollars.[267]

Francis was also involved in an intriguing incident that possibly could have changed the American course of action in Russia. Felix Cole, the Vice Consul at Archangel, wrote a cable, dated June 1, 1918, to Lansing at the State Department. It was an assessment of the situation in Russia. Francis disagreed entirely with Cole's conclusions. Instead of sending the cable to Washington by telegraph, Francis sent it through the postal service causing a delay of some two weeks.[268] During that time, Wilson made his decision to intervene. It will always be questioned if this communiqué would have changed Wilson's mind; nor do we even know if Wilson ever saw the cable.

Cole's cable explained a number of the problems. The first and foremost would be the number of troops needed to be effective in the vastness of this far away country. Piggybacked on this problem was the eventual evacuation problem; as much as eight months of the year the White Sea was frozen. Also, there were the logistics of feeding not just the American soldier, but also the Russians who would help the allied cause. As soon as the Allies arrived, the Bolsheviks would halt all food shipments, Cole believed, to that area. Second, Cole was very concerned that the predicted mass defection to the Allied cause would not happen. The soldiers and peasants were not interested in the Allied "cause." They wanted peace and something to eat - exactly what the Bolsheviks were offering. Cole was also concerned that the Russians would see the entire operation as an occupation of their land by imperialists. Cole's answer to the Russian problem was :

> How can we assist Russia? The best way is through economics. The war after the war is of the utmost importance to the Allies. Russia is backwards and under the insane economic antics of the Bolsheviks. We must make Russia independent of Germany by providing machinery and factories, agricultural implements, and by purchasing excess grain before Germany can get hold of it. We will profit more by using grain, sugar, and machinery than the use of two-hundred thousand troops. . . . The time for soldiers has passed, the time for merchandise is now.[269]

Brigadier General Wilds P. Richardson, Commander of the American troops in Archangel, directed Captain H. S. Martin to prepare a memorandum giving his observations concerning the situation in North Russia. These initially classified documents reported that:

> Our force was too small. . . . Instead of demonstrating to the Russians our strength and instilling into them a spirit of enthusiasm thereby arousing them from the passive [ways], we demonstrated to them our weakness and instilled into them a spirit of disappointment and doubt. . . . The real truth was, we were waging war against Bolshevism. Everybody knew that. Yet no allied government ever stated that that was its policy in intervening. Before the signing of the armistice it was easy to say that we were fighting the allies of Germany. After the armistice, however, when the heaviest fighting of the North Russian campaign took place − we were left in the embarrassing attitude of trying to interpret the policies of our respective governments so as to justify our military activities in Russia. . . . The result was that in the course of a day the ordinary soldier would hear any number of varying and sometimes contradictory replies to the questions which were constantly being asked: for example, why were they called upon to fight the Bolsheviks when they had been mobilized to fight Germany; what were our reasons for making war on the Bolsheviks; why not let Russia take care of her own internal

affairs, etc. . . . In my opinion, ordinary American will never show an enthusiastic military spirit while serving under the immediate command of a foreign officer- particularly under the British. I would say, therefore, in conclusion, that our North Russian expedition lacked that unity of spirit which might have brought forth more favorable results.[270]

Here was a sad summation of the entire affair: lack of commitment; lack of communication; and a lack of concern for the American soldier.

The Polar Bears felt all of this first hand. John Dalian, an American soldier who served in North Russia said, "I hope some day the people in the States get [the] real story and the truth about this awful situation." He was confused as to why he was fighting a war in Russia while the rest of the world celebrated the end of the World War.[271] Other soldiers expressed similar feelings: Edwin L. Arkin stated that, "The little American contingent. . . never knew why they went and never yet had been told."[272] Gordon W. Smith recalled that it was a "frozen Hell," and that they "were forgotten by our own country, ignored by the one for which we were fighting. . . .[while] America was congratulating itself for a great victory and peace."[273] Rodger Sherman Clark wrote to his parents that, "The North Russian Expedition has been a farce from the start, even more a blunder. Pig headedness and lack of foresight characterized all tactics."[274] Almost every "Polar Bear" either wrote or would later recount, how disorganized the entire operation was. They also felt an overwhelming sense of doom because of the lack of communication and proper treatment. L.P. Keith sent home a poem he wrote that seemed to echo the feelings of many:

In December and January are only a few hours of feeble shading light, then tragic blackness blots out the snows and the mournful woods and the skies of the melodrama. With night the tiny windows are shrouded with broad coverings and candles flickering in the low

> ceiling room. . . . Through the long unwholesome hours, the
> Americans sit and think thoughts more black than the outside night.
> . . . Black thoughts of their country and the smug pompous statesmen,
> who with sonorous patriotic phrases, had sent them to exile.[275]

Soon to be one hundred years "young", Polar Bear Ed Karkou remembers the desperation of it all: "We didn't have very much to eat. . . .We had a man in charge [of getting the food]. . . .He would get around in villages, and such, trying to find [food]. . . . One time the men found a sheep. . . . So they stuck a long wood thing through its body and it was roasted. Sunday morning, spring of the year, and by God, we had food! Meat, unusual." He recalls, with a chuckle, he even ate horse meat and "it wasn't bad." He also had a dislike for the British. "You know the British had a lot of liquor. They had one building just full of liquor. We never got much of it, but they sure did."[276] Richard Patching's father shared with him that, "He was scared most of the time and hungry most of the time. . . .He damn near starved to death. . . .He hated the British . . .[the Americans were] sort of sacrificial."[277] Mrs. Stevenson recalled the experience of her father, Lawrence Simpson: "He had very bad memories. Once, he broke down and cried when he recounted when this lieutenant, he greatly admired the man. . . . He said he was on a patrol. . . and the Bolsheviks [attacked] and some [of the men] were wounded and he told his men to take off and he would hold them off. . . . With his revolver and shells and bodies around him he made every bullet count. And when they finally over took him they disemboweled him and hung him up." She also repeated her father's words about the British: "They took the choice meats too and gave what was left over [first] to the Canadians." She said her father was convinced that the only way the Polar Bears made it back to the United States was the large number of parents and loved ones who demanded Congress to return their men home.[278] Sue Saunders' uncle was Sergeant Edward P. Trombley of Company A, 339th Infantry. She recalled that her uncle, "hated the British. . . and they just wanted people [back in the States] to hear what was happening in their own words." Mr. Trombley's father was one of the parents who sent letters to his Congressmen that demanded his son's return. Saunders read the reply that Mr. Trombley got from a Mr. Gilbert A. Currie, House of Representatives: "My. Dear Mr. Trombley, Your telegram of the 31st. just received. . . .Everything possible being done to secure relief of our soldiers in Russia under British command. War Department advises reports greatly exaggerated. . . .It appears all troops in Russia are under British command and nothing can be done by the War Department. This question has been taken up with the British officials. You may depend upon it that every effort will be made to relieve our soldiers in Russia. The War Department has also assured me that conditions in Russia are greatly exaggerated."[279] This communiqué would seem to indicate that the men in Congress were also in the dark about what was happening. John Dalian's father was a member of the Headquarters Company 339th Infantry. He recalled his father's words that, "The British just treated them like garbage. They were lucky to get enough to eat. . . .They had to hunt for wild life."[280]

Colonel George E. Stewart, the Regimental Commander, gave a reason as to why the men were fighting in Russia that many of the soldiers quoted in their diaries: "Americans were fighting in Russia chiefly because they would be annihilated if they didn't fight." Colonel Stewart said he could not give another explanation because he could not get an answer from Washington.[281] Not a very encouraging answer!

Others would add their comments in later years: United States Army Chief of Staff General Peyton C. March, who was present at the White House meeting to hear Wilson read the *Aide Memoire*, called the idea "a serious military mistake." Robert Lansing, then-Secretary Of State, called it that nation's "black period of terrorism."[282] Colonel House stated that a solution to the Russian situation was impossible because no one wanted to deal with Lenin.[283] He felt the Bolsheviks were in control because they represented the simple demand of the peasants – the redistribution of land. Andrew Soutar, a reporter who accompanied General Ironside to Russia stated that, "Many felt it was a private war against the Bolsheviks but nothing could be further from the truth. . . . We were not fighting Bolshevism."[284] Lastly, the official remarks by the Deputy Commissioner of the American Red Cross in Russia summarized the situation: "The Allied forces in North Russia have been seriously mismanaged because of the inefficiency of the [British] High Command." The report further condemned the American command by saying, " The American regimental commander, Colonel Stewart. . . accepts without protest conditions imposed upon his forces by the British High Command which are detrimental to the maintenance of the morale of his regiment. . . . Colonel Stewart remains habitually at Archangel and rarely visits the bulk of his command, which is scattered in small outpost detachments over a wide area."[285] Stewart was frustrated and depressed; the American's looked to him for encouragement and direction and he could only refer them to the British command:

> These forces. . . were shifted about by the British Generals and Colonels and majors often without any information whatever to Colonel Stewart, the American commanding officer. He lost touch with his battalion and company commanders.... He had a discouraging time even in getting his few general orders distributed to the American troops. No wonder that often an American officer or soldier reporting in from a front by order or permission of a British field officer, did not feel that American Headquarters was his real headquarters....We must say candidly that the doughboy came to look upon American Headquarters in Archangel as of very trifling importance in the strange game he was up against....and they blamed their commanding officer, Colonel Stewart....[286]

Reports written about World War I by the United States Army rarely mention information about the Russian expedition. What information is given is very brief and vague in nature. Most often General Pershing is quoted as saying the Americans were sent to Russia to "secure the ports and save the supplies." He also stated that the forces in Russia had minor engagements with Bolshevik forces, with no mention of casualties.[287] Even historians have a hard time with the facts as is evident when George F. Kennan wrote that the Americans had "no part in any actions other than ones of a defensive nature."

Kennan has written several books and articles on Russian foreign affairs with many illuminating insights. He is of the opinion that the efforts in Russia consisted of a "series of confused and uncoordinated efforts, almost negligible in scale, lacking in any central plan." Kennan also suggests that the intervention was a "shock" to the Bolshevik command and it caused "suspicion" and "contempt" of the "capitalist" world. The Allies, according to Kennan, permanently caused the "severe" dictatorship that would rule for decades.[288] Kennan made a scathing indictment on Wilson while reviewing the intervention aftermath:

> By failing, in this way, to follow through on the implementation of his own decision, the President contrived to get the worst of all possible worlds: he irritated the British and French with his *obiter dicta* and drew onto himself, ultimately, the blame for the failure of the entire venture (on the grounds that the United States contribution had been too little and too late); he did not prevent the United States units from being used for precisely the purposes for which he said they should not be used; nor did he withdraw them, as he said he would, when they were thus used; yet he did prevent them from having any proper understanding of the purposes for which they were being used; finally, he rendered the United States vulnerable to the charge, which Soviet propagandists have never ceased to exploit, of interfering by armed force in Soviet domestic affairs.[289]

Many authors agree with Kennan on his latter comments. There is disagreement, however, with his assertion that the intervention was "negligible" and resulted in few casualties. E. M. Halliday says, however, that, "the record ... speaks otherwise."[290] Halliday agreed that the campaign in North Russia was minor compared to the over-all scope of the war; however, he succinctly pointed to the severity of the fighting itself: "The rate of battle casualties there was somewhat lower than it was for American troops in France during World War I, yet the conditions under which the fighting took place were often far more severe: they were, in fact, fantastic."[291]

Other authors, after years of investigations, yield similar views. Scholar Louis Fischer believed the Bolsheviks could have easily been defeated, however, there were not enough supplies left in Archangel to merit even the small force that was sent. He asserts the Allies' presence only caused distrust that would linger for years.[292]

Author D. F. Flemming also asserted that the intervention caused "suspicion" of the Western intentions – and would cause a "strengthened" Bolshevik rule. Flemming concluded by saying, "To us, it was a far away and exotic incident, to them it was flesh and blood. . . . They can not forget, we can."[293]

E. M. Halliday began his research on the intervention because this incident in history, "has been oddly neglected even by professional historians." He surmised that, "the romantic appeal of the word 'Siberia'" focused attention on the American army that was sent to that region. Everyone seemed to have forgotten the men in northern Russia even though the "American troops in Siberia, by way of contrast, never fought against the Red Army."[294] Halliday referred to the intervention as the "tragic first chapter of the relations between the two great powers of the twentieth century." He also made note that President Wilson's demand that the Americans only be used to guard the military stores was "utterly lost upon the British."[295]

Misconceptions of the intervention have existed over the years because of discrepancies in some of the material printed on the subject. Fred W. Neal wrote in the 1960's that, "invasion of Russia and Siberia by the United States and other capitalist countries at the time of the Bolshevik Revolution," caused the animosity that has continued to fester between the two countries. This is not true on two counts: First, the United States did not invade Russia. The British were asked to intervene in the civil war by the Russian White Army – the Americans were committed, Wilson believed, to help an ally. This might be a moot point, but defensible. Second, the American forces arrived ten months after the Bolshevik uprising, therefore were not involved in the revolution.

The American commander who oversaw the withdrawal of American forces from northern Russia, General Richardson, also presented an inaccurate picture. He wrote that prior to the British arrival, the local populace had revolted against the Bolshevik leadership and established a provisional government that would favor British help.[296] This would seem to indicate that the Russian people, in general, were hoping for outside intervention. What General Richardson does not mention is Britain's major involvement in the uprising, with very little help from the peasants. This story is well documented in other writings.

It is also accurate to say that the Soviet Union portrayed an unjust view of the American part in the intervention. Historian Kennan reviewed Soviet historiography when commenting on a Soviet work entitled, "Concerning the Role of the Imperialists of the U.S.A. in Carrying Out the Intervention in the U.S.S.R. in the Years 1917-1920," by S. F. Naida. Naida claimed that the United States' intentions were to turn Russia into an American colony and that the American soldiers were sent to destroy the Bolshevik government in its infancy. The thirty-five page article portrays the United States as the initiator of the entire campaign.[297] He further added that the United States promised food and supplies for Russia if Russia stayed in the war against Germany. After the promise was given, according to Naida, it was never kept. Even if the United States offered food to the Russian people to stay in the war (most scholars disagree with Naida's contention), once the Bolsheviks came to power those promises would have been moot.

Nikita Khrushchev, while visiting the United States in 1959, angrily claimed that if there had not been an Allied intervention, there would not have been a Russian Civil war. He asserted that the Allies tried to destroy the revolution in its very beginning. He argued that, "Russian soldiers have never been on American soil in anger, but American soldiers have been on Russian soil, these are facts." Yes, the Americans did rest on Russian soil, but not in anger; at least not toward the Russian people. The anger, expressed in countless letters and diaries from the Polar Bears, was directed toward the British, for the most part. Pity was felt for the Russian peasant.

Scholars, historians and authors, almost without exception, agree that the Allied intervention in Russia was a total failure and it did more harm than good. All the reasons given for the intervention quickly vaporized; and it left American soldiers stranded in Russia, weary of the American decision making process. The re-establishment of the Eastern Front did not happen; the peasant rebellion against the Bolsheviks did not happen; the Russians automatically finding the solutions to their problems in an Allied victory over Germany (as if mystically) did not happen; and finally, the military supplies stored at Archangel were ultimately abandoned. None of these reasons were ever officially given to the American soldier fighting on this frozen tundra, but when all the mentioned reasons failed, the Polar Bears were still there wondering why they had been forgotten.

What did the United States have to gain from participating in the venture? The answer is unequivocally, nothing. The intervention was developed through a crisis-oriented management style. The one overriding factor during this time in history for the United States, and its Allies, was the defeat of Germany. When factors arose that were not directly connected to the fight on the Western Front, decisions were made quickly and, regrettably, with little regard to long term consequences. Articles have been written regarding the questionable motives of Great Britain and France in the intervention, i.e., hatred of Bolshevism and economic possibilities. However, the United States had nothing to gain from this venture. Kennan writes, ". . . President Wilson - acting reluctantly, against his own better judgment and that of his military advisers, and only with a view to conciliating the European Allies. . . acquiesced to the Allies".[298]

With nothing to gain short term, the United States risked the long term relations with the newly formed Bolshevik Government. The result would be mistrust and bitterness between the United States and the Soviet Union for the next seventy-five years. The intervention was not the only reason for the Cold War that followed, however, it was a significant contribution. Whereas the incident was forgotten by most Westerners as the years passed, it remained a part of Soviet schooling for many years to come.

Was the Soviet historian, Naida, correct in placing the blame at the feet of the United States? The answer, again, is unequivocally, no. The United States was not the principle aggressor in Russia. The American contingent was placed under the command of the British to attack Bolshevik positions. The American forces were following British orders, orders that contradicted Wilson's expressed commands.

Wilson, to be sure, was in the midst of a great carnage never before witnessed in history, however, he assumed that once his orders were given, he need not look back. Wilson thought, "that he had merely to give the general political line on a given question and things would then flow automatically, without further attention on his part."[299] Granted, this mistake on Wilson's part was just one of many that contributed to the Soviet view point. However, there is not a single piece of evidence that would collaborate the view that the United States government at any time called for the overthrow of the Bolshevik government.

What Wilson called for was a democratic partner in Russia that would contribute to a peaceful world. The peasants in Russia, however, were not interested in what Wilson considered important; they wanted peace and, most of all, something to eat.

The blame for the unfortunate participation in northern Russia falls on many. Most of the blame, however, must be placed squarely on President Wilson's shoulders. It was his decision, against the wishes of many of his advisors, to send the troops; his decision to limit the number to a bare minimum; his decision to allow the British to take command; his decision to keep them in Russia after the war was over; and probably the worst of his decisions was not to concern himself with the enactment of his orders. It is easy to say, "the buck stops here," but many times circumstances dictate directions, and blame can not and should not be summarily placed. However, the Northern Russia odyssey leaves most of the blame pointed in one direction – at the "top". It was a huge mistake in an era when most Americans believed that their government would "always" do what was right. The leaders in Washington, the public believed, would explore every avenue, consider every advantage and disadvantage, and then decide what was morally correct for the country. To do otherwise would be unthinkable. As the Polar Bears finally marched home, the American people began to question that assumption.

As many historians have said, the intervention "was a sad and tragic mistake." It was sad and tragic because of the waste of human life, soldiers dying and feeling forgotten for an unknown cause. It reflected poor judgement in the long term, because it contributed heavily to the suspicion and hostile relations between the Soviet Union and the United States. When it was all over, the Polar Bears marched out of Archangel, and, after a time, the Bolsheviks marched in; the peasants received "the conquerors with as much enthusiasm as they had shown the Allies eighteen months before."[300] The peasants wanted only what most people want – peace. It was a sad and tragic ending that tarnished the integrity of the United States in the eyes of much of the world, for years to come. It is also morosely ironic that President Wilson sent his troops to preserve the integrity of Russia, but lost our own integrity in the process. The United States involvement in Russia was a blink in the eye of history. Unfortunately for the United States, it produced a black eye that just now may be healing. A sad and tragic ending, indeed.

CHAPTER VI

THE EPITAPH:

STILL NO ANSWERS

They were in a strange country, fighting an undeclared war under
foreign officers, with unfamiliar weapons and for an uncertain
cause.... They felt – and many still do – that they were rented out to
the British government.
                    –Stanley Bozich, Curator, Michigan's Own, Inc.

The return from North Russia does not end the story of the Polar Bears. The

story lives on in the hearts and minds of all the relatives of these brave and

courageous men. "They loved their country, and were ready to die for it," recounted

Harry Mead's son, Hudson.[301] "My uncle [Edward P. Trombley] instilled in me the

honor and privilege of being able to live in this country" echoed Sue Saunder.[302]

Gregg Ponke wrote about his grandfather, Cpl. Larry Simpson: "When I served in

the army. . . my grandfather wrote me a letter saying how he fought the communists

back in World War I. I had a feeling inside of me I think that he had 50 years ago.

. . . My grandfather helped to make me proud to be an American."[303] The Polar Bears

fought and died in a land that most Americans knew nothing about. While in that

land, they had bitter confrontations not only with the enemy, but with the arctic

darkness, temperatures of fifty below zero, terrain of waist-deep snow, jam prone

weapons calibrated in Russian paces instead of yards, lack of food, and the constant

battle with the British over everything. But when they arrived home, they were very

proud of their accomplishment: the accomplishment of fighting for their country and

surviving under extreme difficulties. Sgt. Matthew G. Grahek, the most decorated

119

man in the 339th having received the United States Distinguished Service Cross and numerous other medals explained, "We had to fight to save our necks and that's what we did. We didn't know why we were fighting the Bolsheviks. We fought to stay alive."[304] Stories would be told and re-told of the events during those few short months in their lives. For many of the returning troops, those months would become the cornerstone of their identity for the rest of their lives.

They would remember with some bitterness, but most of their memories would be filtered through darkened glasses that concealed the pain and recalled the camaraderie and heroism of their fellow troopers. For the rest of their lives they would share these stories to anyone who would listen. Their excitement, patriotism, and courage would become a part of their families' heritage and this would be passed down through future generations. To this day, the families are eager to retell the exploits to a world that still knows very little about the United States' endeavors into Russia. They are also convinced that without the formation of Detroit's Own Welfare Committee, and the constant demands they made upon Congress and the President, fewer of the Polar Bear dough boys would have returned home safely. Many would agree with this assertion.

Seventy-seven years ago a very different America waded into the first catastrophe of the twentieth century. At a time when public discord against the government was considered unpatriotic or at best bad manners, these families demanded and convinced a government that was undecided and a public that was preoccupied, that the fighting in Russia should stop. This small group of grieving Americans, more than any other single person, group or circumstance, single-handedly forced the American Government to make a political foreign policy change. It was the beginning of a new American age; the realization that the government was not always right. But this sort of change comes slowly and is recognized only in retrospect. Novelist Andrew Holleran succinctly recognized this when he said, "No one grows old in a single day." It was one step in the incremental changes to come.

One of the last living Polar Bears, at this writing, is Ed Karkou. He celebrated his 100th birthday on December 9, 1995. He resides alone in a modest size, nicely decorated home in Pontiac, Michigan. His youthful looks and keen awareness of mind deceive the time clock. He is truly shocked that anyone still cares about his exploits in World War I and is extremely excited to talk about the Polar Bears. He, like others who are now gone, remembered the hardships; but for seventy-seven years he also has carried in his heart the honor that he represented his country. His vivid memories center not on the blood and guts of war but on patriotism and the enduring friendships that would last a lifetime. Ed Karkou, like Cleo Colburn, told of the heroism of their comrades and the camaraderie that was formed, especially when they thought the United States government had forgotten them – they thought they might all die together. Ed, Cleo, and the many family members of other Polar Bear veterans conveyed the excitement of the returning soldiers. One obvious reason for euphoria was that they did not die as they feared they would – the motif of the campaign was one of survival, and they made it! As they would later ponder, it was an awesome trip; men who had not gone beyond fifty miles from their homes in their entire lives, had traveled to New York, England, and then on to Russia. The mostly unschooled farmers, storekeepers, and merchants of Michigan had come back as world travelers versed on international affairs. They had stories to tell that were far different than those already told by the troops returning from France. Theirs was a unique experience that would be enthusiastically shared from generation to generation.

There are similar stories in American history; the spring of 1995 marked the example of another poignant event in the history of American foreign policy. April 30 of that year was the 20th anniversary of the American withdrawal from Vietnam. The Vietnam war and the Russian intervention are similar stories that point to the same conclusion; getting involved in another country's conflict at its moment of revolutionary transformation can be devastating. One can "win" only by destroying the enemy, and we were not ready to do that in either Vietnam or Russia. The half-hearted attempt by the United States, in both cases, caused immeasurable harm and grief for years to follow.

A Headquarters detachment of the 339th was the first section to reach Detroit on Thursday at 12 noon July 3, 1919. Major J. Brooks Nichols, commander of the 339th Infantry detachment, made it a point to repeat that he wanted the public to know what actually happened to his men in Russia and that, "the men coming tonight rank with the best troops in America."[305]

July 3, 1919 was a day of great joy for Detroit. At 7:30 p.m. men and officers of A and L Companies, the Medical and Headquarters detachments began arriving. The second section consisted of two trains, arriving at 8:30 p.m. It carried E and I Companies and part of G Company. The third section consisting of M Company, the rest of G Company, and the Machine Gun Company arrived at 11:00 p.m. Each contingent was met by hordes of well-wishers and bands playing repeated tributes to these Detroit heroes. The group of soldiers, upon seeing the awaiting throngs, threw their caps into the sky, acting "generally like boys at the beginning of a vacation. . . . The sounds of cheers, crying and applause went on uninterrupted into the late evening and early morning."[306] The soldiers hugged anyone they could get their arms around, while tears flowed down their faces, bronzed and hardened from the rigors of the winter winds. The tears gushed from tired eyes that saw more than eyes should ever see.

Detroit newspapers reported the great party in the city and tried to summarize what had taken place: There was a universal feeling of pride (for these men). . . who wrote into American military annals the one chapter singular for it's uniqueness and individuality. For no other American troops had served, like them, in the white cold misery of the arctic circle to fight America's battles. It was the city's show of respect for the only American troops assigned to duty at the top of the world in the allied attempt to save Russia from Bolshevism, who incidentally, made up the bulk and backbone of the expedition. It was the city's show of sympathy for the only American troops for whom the armistice signing meant nothing, for whom November 11, 1918 and the days that followed it into 1919 just meant more cold and hardships, more hunger and fighting. So the welcome was to be spontaneous and heartfelt. It was to be simple. There were to be no formalities that tired without pleasing, no parades that delighted only the spectators, no ceremonies to bore those for whom they are intended. The plans provide that the welcomed should be entertained, not the welcomers.[307]

The newspapers were right when stating the Polar Bears had not and would never celebrate November 11, 1918 as the end of the war. Their time of celebration began July 4, 1919.

On the morning of July 4th, the men gathered to board the ferry *Britannia*. It took them to the parade cite on Belle Isle. The trip down the Detroit River was filled with continuous blasts of boat and factory whistles coming from all directions. A speed launch containing the Mayor and his committee escorted the ferry to its destination. Pomp and ceremony was not lacking on the island. As the soldiers stepped onto the shore, rockets were sent into the air signaling the barrage of balloon streamers and flowers. Women and young girls representing the American Red Cross lined the pier showering their heroes with perfumed flower reefs. "From there they paraded around the island past incomputable thousands, past families that craned necks and cried out 'there he is Ma,' and finally to the great quadrangle. . . at the foot of the island."[308]

Mayor James Couzens was the main speaker; his speech was wonderfully crafted and worthy of repeat. It spoke of gallantry and the essence of the making of a hero; it was a lasting tribute to those who fought in the land of Russia. Many times speeches contain undue accolades – not so in this one. Couzens proclaimed to the Regiment these words:

> On this great Victory Fourth, Detroit and Michigan salutes the men of the 339th. We at home may have only a vague conception of the Dvina, the fight at Shenkursk or the Archangel-Vologda Front, but for us you have made the numerals 339 the title of a long-to-be-remembered Michigan epic. They are no longer the mere badge of an Infantry Regiment of the United States Army. They symbolize, in our minds, a story of magnificent endurance, sacrifice and obedience.
>
> You fought under the greatest of all odds. You fought against doubt and an unknown enemy. Yours was none of the spectacular fighting of the red-hot battle line in the Argonne. You battled, figuratively and literally, in the dark and bleakness of a frozen wilderness. You fought on and on against a miserable foe, without the knowledge that you were succeeding, only knowing that you were there to hold that base. You fought doubts in your own hearts; doubt that Headquarters remembered your predicament; that the folks at home knew whether you still lived, that they had received your letters, that relief could ever reach you through the ice-locked sea. Your victory was a triple one – over self pity, discouragement, and the enemy. Only real men win in struggles such as yours. Today you are home again among your loved ones, having lived up to the very highest traditions of the American Army, and we thrill with a new and greater pride at the words, 'Detroit's Own.' Of all Detroit's thousands of returning heroes,

there are none who come back to us having set a better example of patriotism or a higher standard of American manhood. Your story in the black type of history will be one to inspire more than those of this generation.

We people of Detroit, and Michigan, congratulate you and your brave commander Major J. Brooks Nichols, and pledge you our utmost support in reinstating yourselves in civil life.[309]

The soldiers and citizens who listened that day to Mayor Couzens' speech, considered it his finest.

What happened to some of the players of the intervention in later years? "Of the 5,500 members of the American Expedition to North Russia, few ever reached prominence."[310] Probably the most notable exception was General Ironside. He went on to become the governor of the impressive British fort at Gibraltar. Under the General's direction, the Gibraltar City Council built a number of large air raid shelters in various parts of the city. He would later be promoted to Field Marshal, and then to a final promotion to Chief of the Imperial General Staff (CIGS), and Commander in Chief Home Forces. He became a close friend of Winston Churchill. He later was involved heavily in World War II by designing the defense of Great Britain against German invasion. Another possible exception was John Cudahy. Cudahy became President Franklin Roosevelt's Ambassador to Poland. In 1924 he wrote a book on this adventure called, *Archangel: The American War with Russia.* The memory of this ordeal would last a lifetime for Cudahy as he named his only daughter Tulgas, after the battle fought in Russia on Armistice Day.[311]

Ambassador Francis resigned as Ambassador to Russia and spent much of his remaining life believing, and trying to convince others, that his plan for Russia would have worked. He died in 1926. Colonel Stewart was not heard from again, except in the unflattering recollections of some of the soldiers. Stewart seemed the perfect choice to command the expedition. The 46-year-old career soldier won the Medal of Honor in the Philippine campaign in 1900 and also won a battlefield commission. Much has been said about Stewart; weak, unpopular, seldom inspecting the front, never rewarding the bravery of his soldiers and refusing to challenge British authority. It is also a sad commentary that the United States government would put anyone in such a position of non-authority and then relieve him of command just two months before the troops were sent home. True, a stronger man might have represented himself and his unit in a better light, but this was not the case, and Stewart is relegated to unflattering obscurity.

Three other officers of the 339th Infantry wrote a book, in 1920, on the intervention. Captain Joel R. Moore of Company M, Lieutenant Harry H. Mead of Company A, and Lieutenant Lewis E. Jahns were the listed authors of *The History of the American Expedition Fighting the Bolsheviki.* It had the great advantage to be written while the events were still fresh in their minds. It was a well documented, detailed account of the entire event. It was "reverently" dedicated to the men who were wounded or killed in northern Russia.

Moore and Mead were the early presidents of the Polar Bear Association formed in 1922 to continue the bonds of friendship. Joseph Taube recalled, "It was an awful time. It was tolerable only because of our comradeship. When we came home, we wanted to keep the friendships. So we formed the Polar Bear Association (PBA)."[312] One of the major accomplishment of the association was persuading the Michigan State legislature to appropriate $15,000 and Congress to appropriate $80,000 (some accounts put the total appropriation at $200,000)[313] to finance a trip back to Russia to recover the bodies the left behind.

Here, again, it seemed to the "Bear" family members that their government would, once again, conveniently forget those that were still in Russia. This bothered not only the relatives of the abandoned dead but it also took much of the joy away from the returning troops. The Polar Bears were beginning to feel frustration and anger at their government; the same feelings that the family members had experienced. This problem formed a topic of agitation during many of the Association's future meetings. Once again, Michigan congressmen actively got involved, and in the spring of 1929 Senator Arthur Vanderberg pushed through the appropriation bill.

The Soviet Union and the United States did not recognize each other, therefore no direct dealings through diplomatic channels were available. Five volunteers of the Michigan Veterans of Foreign Wars received permission from Moscow to enter Russia as a private party; they would be sent as representatives. Over a three month period, the five man mission recovered eighty-six bodies, sixteen of whom could not be identified. The majority of these were sent back to Michigan and forty-five of the bodies were sent to White Chapel Cemetery in Troy, Michigan. Of the sixteen unidentified bodies, seven were sent to White Chapel. The Cemetery had donated the plot. One other Polar Bear who had been returned in 1919, Harold Maybaum, was also buried there at the request of his family. A funeral procession in December of 1929, with fifty five hearses, was the longest procession in the history of Detroit. Governor Green presided over the elaborate ceremony in Detroit and Col. George Stewart was the Grand Marshal. By the time the first vehicle arrived at the cemetery, some 15 miles away, the last car was leaving Detroit. The Air national guard had a "fly over" in honor of these fallen heroes.

In searching for the bodies in 1929, the person in charge, Walter Dundon writes that since food was scarce in Russia, the group used food as pay for the Russians' help.[314] One Russian reportedly said, "What a wonderful place America must be to send men away over here for dead people."

Dundon also remembered that some United States Senators did not want any of the bodies brought back and used a Theodore Roosevelt quote, "Let the body lie where it may fall." Once the United States government decided to act, great homage was made for its fallen citizens. "Although the living veterans of the AEFNR had returned to the United States in 1919 without any great fuss being made over them, at least before they reached Detroit, the scant relics of the dead late-comers were accorded meticulous homage all the way from France to the White Chapel Cemetery."[315] They were given an honor guard to the ship, *President Roosevelt,* and greeted by a seventeen-gun salute in the United States. A funeral train took most of the bodies to Detroit and three were sent to Arlington National Cemetery. In 1934, Stalin allowed 9 more American bodies to be released. They were buried at White Chapel. A total of fifty-six soldiers are buried around the Polar Bear monument. Those who have died since the end of the war in Russia have been buried along side their comrades. Fourteen bodies were never to be found. Fourteen Americans will always be buried in the frozen tundra of northern Russia.

Time has taken its toll; the association was disbanded a number of years ago when activities were no longer feasible. However, each year on Memorial Day, services are conducted at the White Chapel Cemetery, where many of the relatives still gather. A monument, a magnificent white marble polar bear commemorating those who died in Russia, was dedicated on Memorial Day, 1930. The base of the monument, representing a fortress, is black marble, surmounted by a white marble sculpture of a fierce-looking polar bear standing in snow, with a helmet and cross at its feet to indicate a war burial. The inscription on the base of the granite quotes naval war hero Stephen Decatur; "Our country in her intercourse with Foreign Nations, may she always be in the right, but our country, right or wrong." A young boy, 12 year old Donald McDonald unveiled the monument. His father was Angus

McDonald who died about eight days after he arrived in Russia with Spanish Influenza. There were seventy-two Polar Bears who died from this epidemic almost as soon as they arrived in Russia. Donald had never met his father. Buried in a double circle around the Polar Bear monument are fifty-six of the fallen heroes, including Donald's father. In front of the marble Polar Bear is an historical marker written by Stanley Bozich. He tells of writing the words to the marker, only to have the State change his wording. His original words were, "They returned home to Detroit on July 4, 1919, seven months after the war ended." On the other side of the monument it was to read, "There are still fourteen bodies of American and Michigan soldiers buried somewhere in North Russia in unmarked graves." The State changed the wording to read, "They marched on Belle Isle on July 4, 1919. Ninety-four of them were killed in action after the United States decided to withdraw from Russia but before Archangel's harbor thawed." All mention of the war ending, while the killing and suffering was still continuing, was eliminated. Also eliminated was the recognition of the fourteen Americans still buried in Russia.

Unfortunately, if you were to ask anyone today about the identity of the Polar Bears, you would most likely get answers relating to knowledge of the animal species or those that swim in the middle of the winter.

That is why Stan Bozich is such a valuable asset to the memories of all the soldiers who called themselves Polar Bears. It was his "own curiosity" about these men that led him to collect more "Polar Bear" artifacts than any other person or institution in the world.

"I started collecting things fifty years ago when I was eleven. As a kid in 1945 when the soldiers came back from World War II, we, as kids, had a habit called alley-picking. We would go into the alleys behind the homes in Detroit. When many of the soldiers came home they threw away anything that had to do with the war.

Since the trash was put in the alleys, all the kids would go picking through it all – clothing, medals, everything. Since I was the oldest of the group of kids, I got first pick. That's how I started collecting. In 1950, I came across a Polar Bear uniform. This is before I went into the Navy in 1951. I didn't know too much about this group of soldiers but I remembered that my grandfather, a Detroit policeman, had taken me downtown while a Polar Bear convention was in process. The only thing I could remember from that experience is that these were the only men to ever fight in Russia from the United States. When I purchased the uniform, it brought back memories and it intrigued me. I was born and raised in Detroit, and those men were from Detroit; that's what piqued my interest in them. I made up my mind I was going to find out about this group of men. While doing this I was collecting many other war articles and I got to be quite knowledgeable in the fields of collecting. In fact I published a couple of books on the identification of Nazi uniforms, headgear, armbands, daggers, helmets and things. In 1970 I decided I would have a museum on the war crimes of the Nazis. It was the first holocaust museum in the United States. A number of Jewish groups came and were pleased with the dignity and extent of the museum – we had original artifacts. A Jewish group called 'Sharit Haplaytah' (survivors of 1945), would sit on the benches outside the museum testing the reaction of the people as they left. In 1974, the Jewish community, I believe impressed with what we had done, decided to open their own museum. I knew at that time they would be doing a great job. I was actually doing this part time – my full time job was as a Royal Oak, Michigan firefighter (retired in 1987).

In 1974, my wife and I toured the Soviet Union. We spent 22 days there. In every town, city and village throughout the country they had museums honoring their war heroes. The uniforms of their men and women were on display, along with their decorations, and a story of what they did. They are a very patriotic people. It was a very emotional experience and I thought, 'Why don't we exhibit this kind of patriotism in our country? Why don't we have more places to honor our war heroes?' We seem to forget our heroes as soon as the war is over.

"If you recall, in the 1970's a lot of our citizens were still burning American flags and wearing them on the seat of their pants in protest to the Vietnam war and our government. When we got back from Russia, I knew we would be closing the War Crimes museum and I wanted to start a museum similar to those in the Soviet Union. We were the first ones presumptuous enough not only to consider the idea of a Michigan Military Museum, but to actually start tracking down our veterans and asking them for their uniforms. We knew we had the nucleus of a collection with our Polar Bear artifacts because we had nine uniforms at that time. The Russians knew a great deal about the Polar Bears but most Americans did not and still don't. So I concentrated on establishing a new museum. We were living in Sterling Heights, Michigan and in 1980 moved to beautiful Frankenmuth, Michigan. Besides "Bear" items, I traveled around the country tracking down Michigan Medal of Honor recipients. I believed they should be honored in our museum. I also began contacting Michigan astronauts and collecting their uniforms and artifacts as a tribute to them."[316]

Stan Bozich extensively researched books in the local and national archives, newspapers, and magazines, and conducted interviews with innumerable people before opening the door to his museum. It now has the largest collection of Polar Bear artifacts in the world. The museum has more than 50 Polar Bear uniforms plus medals, weapons, letters, diaries, and other artifacts. They also have the largest collection of Medals of Honor on display in the United States (sixteen), even more than the Medal of Honor Society itself. The editor of the Bay City Times recently wrote that Stan Bozich possibly had the best space exhibit he had ever seen; great accolades for a small museum in a small town in Michigan.

Frankenmuth is famous for its chicken dinners, colorful ethnic atmosphere and wonderful intriguing gift shops. It is Michigan's number one tourist attraction because of its quaint Bavarian village atmosphere. The town brings back memories of old charm and "the way it use to be" feelings. This setting is perfect for a museum that does not glorify war; rather, it pays tribute to those who pledged a commitment to their country and made the ultimate sacrifice in the performance of their duty.

Stan Bozich related, "around 1983 they [Polar Bears] started dying off. It was like losing a grandfather a week. I use to pick many of them up to take them to the 'Bear' meetings. They made me an honorary member of the Polar Bear Association in 1980. I was thrilled to death that they felt that way about me and I made them two promises. First of all, there would always be a part of our museum dedicated to them; and second, I would see to it that the Memorial Day services at White Chapel Cemetery in Troy, Michigan would be held every year. I was going to make sure this was done in perpetuity. Every Memorial Day for the past 22 years I'm at White Chapel Cemetery."

When the Polar Bears arrived home they were given a Victory medal that everyone who served in World War I got. On the medal was a brass bar that would show which battles the soldier fought. The Polar Bears came home and were given a medal that said "defensive sector." Mr. Bozich said that "Many of the soldiers were upset and felt insulted by the treatment of their own government." They petitioned the United States government for their own separate medal. The government refused but did agree to issue a new brass bar that replaced the words "defensive sector" with the word "Russia." That pleased many of the soldiers but the insults did not stop. While agreeing to issue the new bar, the government informed them the charge would be $2.00.

At the annual convention held in 1924, there appeared an article entitled, "History of Polar Bears." The article contained these words: Precious American lives were given on the fields of battle in that fall campaign and in the desperate winter campaign that followed. And reluctantly, but valorously, the American soldiers had fought the Russians, taking heavy toll for every verst of ground given up in retreats before overwhelming odds. Ust Padenga, Vistavka, Toulgas, Kitsa, Kodish, Chekuevo, Karpogora, Obozerskaya, Bolshe-Ozerke and numerous small Russian places were scenes of stern battle encounter that reddened the soil and snows with American and Russian Blood.

Heroic deeds and hardships scarce believable make the story of that strange war waged by the Americans up there near the Arctic circle, in swamp and forest, on frozen stream trails and in snow-bound villages and blockhouse defenses.

One in every ten of those Americans, after battle, had found a final resting place under a crude grave cross bearing the sad inscription KIA, or had found a cot in one of the improvised hospitals for wounded. And, in all, over a thousand Americans . . . passed through old Captain Greenleaf's convalescent hospital, which ministered to the wounded, the frozen and the sick, broken by hardships.

From the beginning of this unique event in American history, the soldiers had to endure extremely difficult situations. It started when Michigan farmers arrived at Fort Custer anticipating adequate training for the future fighting in France, and, instead, some were given as little as three weeks training with weapons and tactics that would be discarded when the fighting began. It continued with Presidential orders that were ignored; leaders at the very top of the government frozen in indecision; a change in clothing (to the British cold weather gear); unfamiliar weapons; lack of food; foreign military leaders; being commanded by a foreign government; temperatures that reached 50 degrees below zero; death wards; an enemy estimated at over one million; and never being given a reason for fighting in Russia after the war was over. It ended when they arrived home seven months after the end of the war; wondering among themselves as to why it seemed their own government had forgotten them. Military historian, S.L.A. Marshall said that, "They had to return to remind us they had ever gone. It was as if fate had set herself to mock the whole adventure, tormenting the pride of man by making their trial by ice and fire seem half ridiculous."[317] Their fallen comrades would not be brought back for proper burial and they would be charged $2.00 for their own battle medal.

The United States sent troops to help guard storage depots. The Government insisted that the expedition did not have as its aim the overthrow of the Russian government. However, the result speaks for itself. The war ended and Wilson relented to British pressure to continue the fight against the Bolsheviks. The President's half-hearted attempt to appease the British sent the Polar Bears into a malaise that could only end in death for some and uncertain escape for the others. Wilson's orders were disobeyed, but the guilty parties were not the ones punished; the soldiers themselves suffered the consequences.

The United States government, under Wilson, asked and received much from these men. In return, the soldiers, sad to say, were given only memories to pass on. These memories must not be forgotten, as it is all that they were given in return for their service. The foray into Russia had produced little results. "The allies' effort won them nothing but the lasting suspicion of the communists whose own eventual success deepened Western fears. . . ."[318] Our intervention turned out to be the least useful, least self-serving, and most damaging adventure in America's foreign policy forays. Wilson was persuaded by the idea that intervention would shorten the war, which it did not; and once the war was over we could destroy Bolshevism, which once again, did not happen. His advisors led him astray. "It is . . . doubtful. . . that the war weary peoples of the Western powers could have been persuaded to make the immense effort necessary; and the White Russians who were fighting the Bolsheviks were as far from being democrats as Lenin's followers."[319] It was a fiasco that would haunt the United States for the next seventy years. This small but intense war between Soviet and American soldiers would be the background for what would be called the "cold war."

    With all of the obstacles placed in front of these men, it is truly amazing that most of them made it home alive! They made it home by the grace of God and – "The first day I was in Camp Custer, I picked a four leaf clover. The first day I arrived in New York at Camp Mills on our way to Russia, I picked a four leaf clover. The first day in England, I picked a four leaf clover. After we left the boat, I picked a four leaf clover in Russia. There was four of them that I had picked from the time I left home until we was where the action was. *I just feel I was lucky.*"[320]

APPENDIX A
AIDE MEMOIRE[321]

The whole heart of the people of the United States is in winning this war. The controlling purpose of the Government of the United States is to do everything that is necessary and effective to win it. It wishes to cooperate in every practicable way with the Allied Governments, and to cooperate ungrudgingly; for it has no end of its own to serve and believes that the war can be won only by common counsel and intimate concert of action. It has sought to study every proposed policy or action in which its cooperation has been asked in this spirit, and states the following conclusions in the confidence that, if it finds itself obliged to decline participation in any undertaking or course of action, it will be understood that it does so only because it deems itself precluded from participating by imperative considerations either of policy or of fact.

In full agreement with the Allied Governments and upon unanimous advice of the Supreme War Council, the Government of the United States adopted, upon its entrance into the war, a plan for taking part in the fighting on the Western Front into which all its resources of men and material were to be put, and put as rapidly as possible, and it has carried out that plan with energy and success, pressing its execution more and more rapidly forward and literally putting into it the entire energy and executive force of the nation. This was its response, its very willing and hearty response, to what was the unhesitating judgment alike of its own military advisers and of the advisers of the Allied Governments. It is now considering, at the

137

suggestion of the Supreme War Council, the possibility of making very considerable additions even to this immense program which, if they should prove feasible at all, will tax the industrial processes of the United States and the shipping facilities of the whole group of associated nations to the utmost. It has thus concentrated all its plans and all its resources upon this single absolutely necessary object.

In such circumstances it feels it to be its duty to say that it can not, so long as the military situation on the Western Front remains critical, consent to break or slacken the force of its present effort by diverting any part of its military force to other points or objectives. The United States is at a great distance from the other field of action. The instrumentalities by which it is to handle its armies and its stores have at great cost and with great difficulty been created in France. They do not exist elsewhere. It is practicable for her to do a great deal in France; it is not practicable for her to do anything of importance or on a large scale upon any other field. The American Government, therefore, very respectfully requests its associates to accept its deliberate judgment that it should not dissipate its force by attempting important operations elsewhere.

It regards the Italian Front as closely coordinated with the Western Front, however, and is willing to divert a portion of its military forces from France to Italy if it is the judgment and wish of the Supreme Command to do so. It wishes to defer in all others, particularly because it considers these two fronts closely related as to be practically but separate parts of a single line and because it would be necessary that any American troops sent to Italy should be subtracted from the number used in France and be actually transported across French territory from the ports now used by the armies of the United States.

It is the clear and fixed judgment of the Government of the United States, arrived at after repeated and very searching reconsiderations of the whole situation in Russia, that military intervention there would add to the present sad confusion in Russia rather than cure it, injure her rather than help her, and that it would be of no advantage in the prosecution of our main design, to win the war against Germany. It can not, therefore, take part in such intervention or sanction it in principle. Military intervention would, in its judgment, even supposing it to be efficacious in its immediate avowed object of delivering an attack upon Germany from the east, be merely a method of making use of Russia, not a method of serving her. Her people could not profit by it, if they profited by it at all, in time to save them from their present distresses, and their substance would be used to maintain foreign armies, not to reconstitute their own. Military action is inadmissible in Russia, as the Government of the United States sees the circumstances, only to help the Czecho-Slovaks consolidate their forces and get into successful cooperation with their Slavic kinsmen and to steady any efforts of self-government or self-defense in which the Russians themselves may be willing to accept assistance. Whether from Vladivostok or Murmansk and Archangel, the only legitimate object for which American or Allied troops can be employed, it submits, is to guard military stores which may subsequently be needed by Russian forces and to render such aid as may be acceptable to the Russians in the organization of their own self-defense. For helping the Czecho-Slovaks there is immediate necessity and sufficient justification. Recent developments have made it evident that that is in the interest of what the Russian people themselves desire, and the Government of the United States is glad to contribute the small force at its disposal for that purpose. It yields, also, to the judgment of the Supreme Command in the matter of establishing a small force at Murmansk, to guard the stores at Kola, and to make it safe for Russian forces to come together in organized bodies in the North. But it owes frank counsel to say that it can go no further than these modest and experimental plans. It is not in a position, and has no expectation of being in a position, to take part in organized intervention in adequate force from either Vladivostok or Murmansk and Archangel. It feels that it ought to add, also, that it will feel at liberty to use the few troops it can spare only for the purposes here stated and shall feel obliged to withdraw these forces, in order to add them to the forces at the Western Front, if the plans in whose execution it is now intended that they should cooperate should develop into others inconsistent with the policy to which the Government of the United States feels constrained to restrict itself.

At the same time the Government of the United States wishes to say with the utmost cordiality and good will that none of the conclusions here stated is meant to wear the least color of criticism of what the other governments associated against Germany may think it wise to undertake. It wishes in no way to embarrass their choices of policy. All that is intended here is a perfectly frank and definite statement of policy which the United States feels obliged to adopt for herself and in the use of her own military forces. The Government of the United States does not wish it to be understood that in so restricting its own activities it is seeking, even implication, to set limits to the action or to define the policies of its associates.

It hopes to carry out the plans for safeguarding the rear of the Czecho-Slovaks operating from Vladivostok in a way that will place it and keep it in close cooperation with a small military force like its own from Japan, and if necessary from other Allies, and that will assure it of the cordial accord of all the Allied powers; and it proposes to ask all associated in this course of action to unite in assuring the people of Russia in the most public and solemn manner that none of the governments uniting in action either in Siberia or in northern Russia contemplates any interference of any kind with the political sovereignty of Russia, any intervention in her internal affairs, or any impairment of her territorial integrity either now or hereafter, but that each of the associate powers has the single object of affording such aid as shall be acceptable, to the Russian people in their endeavor to regain control of their own affairs, their own territory, and own destiny.

It is the hope and purpose of the Government of the United States to take advantage of the earliest opportunity to send to Siberia a commission of merchants, agricultural experts, labor advisers, Red Cross representatives, and agents of the Young Men's Christian Association accustomed to organizing the best methods of spreading useful information and rendering educational help of a modest sort, in order in some systematic manner to relieve the immediate economic necessities of the people there in every way for which opportunity may open. The execution of this plan will follow and will not be permitted to embarrass the military assistance rendered in the rear of the westward-moving forces of the Czecho-Slovaks.

Washington, 17 July 1918.

APPENDIX B

CHRONOLOGY

Only a World War I Victory Medal service clasp inscribed, "Russia," was authorized, at the cost of the service men. It covered the service period from November 12, 1918 to August 5, 1919, for those veterans of the Russian conflict. The months of fighting and dying in Russia before Armistice Day were never acknowledged by the government.

Units that were sent:

- 339th Inf. Reg.,
- 310th Engineer Reg., (1st Bn..)
- 337th Ambulance Co.,
- 337th Field Hospital, and
- 167th and 168th R.R. Cos. of the North Russia Transportation Corps.

1918

May 24

Allied troops sent to occupy Archangel to avert the possibility of stockpiled arms and munitions from falling into unfriendly hands. Fifty-five crewmen from the U.S. cruiser *Olympia* participate.

June 11

One hundred fifty U.S. Marines land in North Russia.

143

August 3

Sailors from the *Olympia* go ashore to serve as legation guards. Twenty-five Bluejackets, as part of "B Force," engage in the initial U.S. action of the expedition in Archangel's rail yards. Ensign Donald Hicks, wounded, is the first Allied casualty.

Sept. 4

U.S. forces of the American North Russian Expeditionary Force – 339th Infantry Regiment – land at Archangel. Total: 5,108 soldiers and 720 railway engineers.

Sept. 11

Two platoons of Company M make initial contact with Bolsheviks.

Sept. 16

L and I Companies sustain the first U.S. Army casualties: 3 Killed and 2 Wounded.

Sept. 15-30

In the drive to set up a defensive perimeter at the railroad, connecting the eastern and western shores of the White Sea, U.S. forces suffer more casualties: 48 Killed and 58 Wounded.

Nov.11-14

This battle is now called the Battle of Armistice Day. Along the Dvina River at Toulgas, 28 Allies killed and 70 are wounded. More than 300 Russian dead are counted.

1919

Jan 19

This battle is called the Battle of Ust Padenga. Companies A and C and elements of the 310th Engineers are attacked. U.S. casualties: 27 Killed.

May-Apr 5

This is the last major U.S. engagement of the expedition. It is called the Battle of Bolshie Ozerki. Allies withstand simultaneous frontal and rear assaults during the Red's largest offensive. D and M Companies and elements of E Company fortify blockhouses at Verst 18. H Company holds town's outskirts. Allies inflict 2,000 enemy casualties.

May 30

Last official formation is held on Memorial Day.

June 27

Last U.S. personnel depart. Total U.S. casualties: 137 Killed in action; 305 Wounded in action; 72 Dead from diseases; 9 Killed accidentally.[322]

NOTES

1   Cleo Colburn, Interview. Veteran of World War I and a "Polar Bear".
2.   There were four regiments in the 85th Division: The 337th, 338th, 339th and 340th. The 339th was sent to Russia and the other three sent to France.
3.   Joe Carmichael, *A Short History of the Russian Revolution*, pg. 34.
4.   Hudson Mead, Interview. Father was World War I "Polar Bear."
5.   E. M. Halliday, *The Ignorant Armies*, pg. 218.
6.   Ibid.
7.   J. R. Moore, H.H. Mead, L.E. Jahns, *The American Expedition Fighting the Bolsheviki*, pg. 47.
8.   Colburn, Interview, however, this was not the case. Arrived September4 and Company I, K, L, & M went active on September 5. The first contact happened in November. Mr. Colburn was part of I Company.
9.   *U.S News & World Report*, November 13, 1995, pg. 21.
10.   Albert L. Weeks, *The First Bolshevik*, pg. 9.
11.   Weeks, *The First Bolshevik*, pg. 14.
12.   Ibid., pg. 43.
13.   Ibid., pg. 114.
14.   Leopold H. Haimson, *The Russian Marxists and The Origins of Bolshevism*, Intro.
15.   Ibid., pg. 17.
16.   Dmitri Volkogonov, *Lenin, A New Biography*, pg. 90.
17.   Ibid., pp. 89-95.
18.   Haimson, *The Russian Marxists*, Pg. 45.
19.   Volkogonov, *Lenin*, Pg. 96.
20.   Haimson, *The Russian Marxists*, Pg. 102.
21.   Ibid., Pg. 117.
22.   John W. Wheeler-Bennett, *Brest-Litovsk*, Pg. 18.
23.   Carmichael, *A Short History*. Iron and coal production was also considered, by many, as a chief reason for the English and French intervention.
24.   Alan Moorehead, *The Russian Revolution*, pg. 12.
25.   Volkogonov, *Lenin*, pg. 493.
26.   Totals have varied in different writings, but figures given are accepted by historians.
27.   Carmichael, *A Short History*, pg. 34.
28.   Ibid., pg. 80.
29.   Reader can find fascinating information on this topic by reading, *Last Mystery of the Czar*, by Rudolph Chelminski. Telling account of G. Ryabou and Alexander Avdonin.
30.   Volkogonov, *Lenin*, pg. 490.
31.   United States Department of State, Papers Relating to the Foreign Relations of the United States, 1918, Russia, three vols. Washington D.C.: Government Printing Office, 1931-1932, 1:12. Lansing was Secretary of State from June 1915 to February 1920.

148

32. United States Dept. of State, Papers, 1918, Russia, 1:12. Francis served as Ambassador to Russia from April 1916 to May 1931.
33. United States Department of State, Papers Relating to the Foreign Relations of the United States, 1917, Supplement 2: The World War, Two vols. Washington D.C.: Government Printing Office, 1931, 1:200.
34. Richard Pipes, *Russia Under the Bolshevik Regime*, pg. 491.
35. Richard Pipes, *The Russian Revolution*, pp. 762-763.
36. Moorehead, *The Russian*, pg. 175.
37. Volkogonov, *Lenin*, pg. 409.
38. Page was the Ambassador to Great Britain from April 1913 to November 1918.
39. Robert J. Maddox, *The Unknown War With Russia*, pg. 27.
40. Volkogonov, *Lenin*, pg. 239.
41. Adam B. Ulam, *Expansion and Coexistence: The History of Soviet Foreign Policy, 1917-1967*, pg. 63.
42. D.F. Flemming, *The Cold War and Its Origins: 1917-1960*, Two vol. 1:17.
43. Ray Stannard Baker, *Woodrow Wilson: Life and Letters*, Eight Vol., 7:349.
44. George F. Kennan, *The Decision to Intervene*, pp. 9-10
45. Edwin P. Hoyt, *America's Wars & Military Excursions*, pg. 351.
46. Silas B. McKinley, *Woodrow Wilson*, pg. 212.
47. Ibid., pg. 213.
48. David R. Francis, *Russia From the American Embassy*, pg. 339.
49. United States Dept. of State, *Papers, 1918*, 1:245.
50. Frederick Palmer, *Dewton D. Baker: America at War*, Two vol. 2:313.
51. John J. Pershing, *My Experiences in the Word War*, Volume II, pg. 176.
52. Stanley J.Bozich, *Detroit's Own Polar Bears*.
53. Moore, *The American Expedition Fighting the Bolsheviki*, Pg. 50.
54. Richard Pipes, *The Russian Revolution*, pg. 839.
55. Stanley J. Bozich, *Detroit's Own Polar Bears*, pg. 14.
56. John Bradley, *Allied Intervention in Russia*, pg. 211.
57. George F. Kennan, *Russia and the West under Lenin and Stalin*, pg. 69.
58. United States Department of State, *Papers Relating to the Foreign Relations of the United States, Russia, 1918*, 2:472
59. Dennis Gordon, *Quartered In Hell*, pp. 35-36.
60. Interview with Cleo Colburn, pg. 2.
61. Gordon, *Quartered*, pg. 38.
62. Interview with son of Lieutenant Harry Mead, Hudson Mead, pg. 2.
63. Kennan, *The Decision to Intervene*, pg. 17.
64. Edwin P. Hoyt, *America's Wars & Military Excursions*, pg. 352.
65. Betty Miller Unterberger, *America's Siberian Expedition, 1918-1920*, pg. 28.
66. Unterberger, *America's Siberian*, pg. 6.
67. Ibid., pg.. 65.
68. John Dos Passos, *Mr. Wilson's War*, pg. 374
69. *The Sunday Cleveland Leader*, July 7, 1918.
70. Ibid.
71. Kennan, *The Decision to Intervene*, pg. 418.

72. John J. Pershing, *My Experiences in the World War*, 2 Vol, II, 149.
73. See Appendix A
74. Alexander Trachtenberg, ed., *V.I. Lenin: Collected Works*, 23:90.
75. Bozich, *Detroit's Own*, pg. 20.
76. Richard Kolb, "The Bolo War" *Army*, pp. 70-80.
77. Bozich, *Detroit's Own*, pg. 21.
78. Interview with Stan Bozich, owner of "The Military & Space Museum."
79. A number of these documents can be found at the Bentley Library, U/M.
80. Jay Bonnell, Reminiscences 1919, Manuscripts Bentley Library.
81. Colburn, interview. Colburn seems to be confused. It would eventually get to 52 below zero, but when he arrived in Russia the date was September 4, 1918; the temperature was mild.
82. Richard Bak, *Michigan History* May/June 1988, pp. 40-45.
83. Bak, *Michigan History,* pp. 40-45.
84. Colburn, interview. I have not read another account like this.
85. Halliday, *The Ignorant Armies*, pg. 44.
86. Major General F.C. Poole, commander of the British army and in charge of American troops.
87. Halliday, *The Ignorant Armies*, pp. 43-44.
88. Ibid., pg. 46.
89. Ibid., pg. 47.
90. Ray S. Baker, *Woodrow Wilson: Life and Letters*, 8:325.
91. John Dos Passos, *Mr. Wilson's War*, pg. 395.
92. Christopher Dobson, *The Day They Almost Bombed Moscow*, pg. 126.
93. Ibid., pp. 126-127.
94. Ibid., pg. 126.
95. Halliday, *The Ignorant Armies*, pg. 34.
96. Richard H. Ullman, *Intervention and the War*, pg. 178.
97. Colburn, Interview.
98. Ibid.
99. Stan Bozich, Interview.
100. Halliday, *The Ignorant Armies*, pg. 52.
101. Letter by Rodger Clark to wife, June 1, 1919. Stan Bozich stated, "There just were not any available, unless they got them from the Salvation Army, YMCA, etc."
102. Mechanic Albert Geltz, interviewed by Stan Bozich, July 8, 1980. The flag is displayed at "The Military & Space Museum", in Frankenmuth, Michigan.
103. Rodger Sherman Clar, Papers 1918-1919 Bentley Library.
104. John Dalian's letter home, pp. 15-16.
105. Arkins Collection, AA4611, Bentley.
106. Halliday, *The Ignorant Armies*, pg. 52.
107. Halliday, *The Ignorant Armies*, pp. 154-155.
108. Ibid., pg. 154.
109. United States Department of State, *Papers*, 2:546.
110. Ibid., 2:557.
111. Halliday, *The Ignorant Armies,* pp. 160-161.

112. United States Department of State, *Papers*, 575-577.
113. Halliday, *The Ignorant Armies*, pg. 218.
114. Arkins Collection, AA4611, Bentley Library, U/M.
115. Clark Collection, letter to wife, Bentley Library, U/M.
116. Bak, "Michigan History" pg. 44.
117. Moore, *The American Expedition Fighting Bolsheviki*, pg. 102.
118. Colburn, Interview.
119. Moore, *The American Expedition Fighting Bolsheviki*, pg. 106.
120. Halliday, *The Ignorant Armies*, pp. 11-12.
121. Ibid., pp. 10-11.
122. Stan Bozich's Military & Space Museum in Frankenmuth, Michigan has one of the first original five point Red Star emblem on display.
123. Kolb, "The Bolo War"
124. Godfrey J. Anderson Reminiscences, Bentley Library.
125. Ibid.
126. Cudahy papers, Bentley Library.
127. Roy MacLaren, *Canadians in Russia, 1918-1919*, pg. 58.
128. Kennan, *The Decision to Intervene*, pp. 470-471.
129. *The Detroit News* Saturday February 1, 1919, Page 1. Military & Space Museum archives, Frankenmuth, Michigan.
130. Sergt. Waldo E. Pease, Co K, 339th Infantry Quoted front page *The Detroit News*, January 12, 1919.
131. *The Detroit News*, Friday, January 31, 1919, Page 1. M & S Archives.
132. *The Detroit Free Press*, Sunday, February 2, 1919, Page 1. M & S Archives.
133. Jay G. Hayden's article in *The Detroit News*, Feburary 3, 1919, "339th Peril Becomes Wilson's First Task" Page 1. M & S Archives.
134. *The Detroit Free Press*, February 4, 1919, M & S Archives.
135. Ibid., February 6, 1919. M. & S. Archives.
136. Ibid.
137. Ibid., February, 1919.
138. Ibid.
139. Ibid.
140. Ibid., February 6, 1919.
141. Ibid., February 5, 1919, Paris. M & S Archives.
142. Ibid., February 6, 1919. M & S Archives.
143. Moore, *The American Expedition Fighting The Bolsheviki*, pp. 142-143.
144. *The Detroit News*, February 17, 1919. John P. Coakley. M & S Archives.
145. Ibid., February, 1919.
146. *The Chicago Daily Tribune*, Article by Frazier Hunt, February 10, 1919. M &S Archives.
147. Articles in both *The Detroit News* and *The Detroit Free Press*, February 13, 1919. M & S Archives.
148. Ibid., February 12, 1919.
149. Letter to Editor, *The Detroit Free Press* by Dr. & Mrs. H.W. Powers, Amherst, Lorain county, Ohio. No date shown. M & S Archives.
150. *The Detroit Free Press*, Feburary 14, 1919, Washington D. C. M & S Archives.

151. Ibid.
152. Originals are at the University of Michigan Historical Library.
153. *The Detroit Free Press* Editors box, February, 1919. M & S Archives.
154. *The Detroit News*, February 15, 1919. J.A. Mathrews, Washington, D. C., M & S Archives.
155. *The Detroit Free Press*, February 15, 1919, Washington, D. C. M & S Archives.
156. *The Detroit News*, January 29, 1919. Washington, D.C. M & S Archives.
157. *The Detroit News*, February 17, 1919. Associated Press, Archangel. M & S Archives.
158. *The Detroit News*, February 14, 1919. J.A. Mathews, Washington. M & S Archives.
159. *The Detroit Journal*, February 17, 1919. M & S Archives.
160. *The Detroit News*, February 20, 1919. Titled "339th O.K." M & S Archives.
161. *The Detroit News*, February 18, 1919. Odessa. M & S Archives.
162. *The Detroit Journal*, February 19, 1919. M & S Archives.
163. Ibid., Editorial. M & S Archives.
164. Original program at the M & S Museum.
165. *The Detroit Free Press*, February 22, 1919. Titled "Tell Of Cold 339th Suffers" Comments by John Przybyiski, Company M 339th. M & S Archives.
166. Letters from John Dalian to his parents. Interview with family members.
167. Letters from John W. Cwerwinski to fiance, Miss Dorothy Wejrowski. At UofM Library and printed in *The Detroit Free Press* with no date showing. M & S Archives.
168. M & S Archives.
169. M & S Archives.
170. *The Detroit Journal*, February April 4, 1919. Arthur Sears Henning, "Unfurl That Old U.S. Flag Again! Johnson Calls". M & S Archives.
171. *The Detroit News*, April 5, Washington. "339th Coming Home In June." M & S Archives.
172. *The Detroit Free Press*, "Return 339th Detroit's Plea" April, but no date shown. M & S Archives. All Michigan newspaper carried same Associated Press dispatch, dated April 10.
173. One headline read: "Yanks In Russia Balk At Fighting." M & S.
174. *Literary Digest*, July 12, 1919, "That American Mutiny in Russia."
175. Interview with Cleo Colbun. Also found in letter at U/M Archives.
176. *The Detroit Free Press*, May 1. Front page.
177. The Associated Press, Dated May 20, Titled: "Why U.S. Troops in Russia? Senators Ask."
178. W.P. Richardson, "America's War in Northern Russia" *Current History*, February 1921, 13, 293.
179. Headlines from "Journal Washington Bureau" dated May 24, and *The Detroit Free Press* dated May 24.
180. Bozich, *Detroit's Own*.
181. In 1929 the Michigan State legislature appropriated $15,000.00 and the United States Congress gave $80,000.00 to finance a trip back to Russia to recover the bodies. Russia would not allow any "Polar Bear" Veteran to enter their country, so members of the Veterans of Foreign Wars sent representatives. Over a three month period, the eleven man mission recovered 86 bodies, 26 of which could not be identified. The majority of them, 56, were sent back to Michigan.
182. Editorial, "The Fellowcrafter" 1919, Pg. 5, M & S Archives.
183. Bozich, *Detroit's Own*.
184. Nicholas Wolterstorff, "Daily Devotions From Godly Men."

185. *New York Times*, November 8, 1919, Ftpg.
186. William M. Tuttle, Jr., *Race Riot -Chicago in the Red Summer of 1919*, pg. 19.
187. *New York Times*, November 8, 1919, Pg. 2.
188. Ibid., December 1, 1919, Ftpg.
189. Robert Stauss Feuerlicht, *America's Reign of Terror*, pp. 5-6.
190. Bruce A. Rubenstein, *Michigan A History of the Great Lakes State*, pp.198-199.
191. Ibid., pg. 199.
192. Tuttle, Jr., *Race Riot – Red Summer of 1919*, pg. 14.
193. Robert Conot, *American Odyssey*, pg. 205.
194. J. Edgar Hoover, *Masters Of Deceit*, pg. 53.
195. *New York Times*, February, 18, 1919, Ftpg.
196. Tuttle, Jr., *Race Riot – Red Summer of 1919*, pg. 18.
197. Wilma Henrickson, *Detroit Perspectives-Crossroads and Turning Points*, pg. 299.
198. Conot, *American Odyssey*, pp. 204-205.
199. Frank & Arthur Woodford, *All Our Yesterdays*, pg. 245.
200. Conot, *American Odyssey*, pp. 204-205.
201. Tuttle, Jr., *Race Riot – Red Summer of 1919*, Pg. 17.
202. *New York Times*, January 6, 1919, George Kirkpatrick speaking, Editorial Page.
203. Ibid., January 13, 1919, Editorial Page.
204. Ibid., January 19, 1919, Editorial Page 2.
205. Ibid., January 20, 1919, Editorial Page, "The Bolsheviki and Their Apologists."
206. Ibid., "MME. Breskovskaya Tells Of Russia's Need."
207. Ibid., February 27, 1919.
208. *Syracuse Post-Standard*, July 29, 1919.
209. *New York Times*, February 9, 1919, Ftpg.
210. Feuerlicht, *America's Reign of Terror*.
211. Ibid.
212. Quotes taken from March issues of the *New York Times*.
213. *New York Times*, February 13, 1919, Editorial Page.
214. Ibid., February 14, 1919, Editorial Page.
215. Marilyn Bechtel, *Six Decades That Changed The World: The U.S.S.R After 60 Years*, pg. 87.
216. Ibid., pg. 110.
217. An example of this: *New York Times Magazine*, March 16,1919.
218. *New York Times*, March 28, 1919.
219. Stanley Washington of New Jersey, *New York Times*, March 4, 1919. Charles MacKean of Philadelphia, *New York Times*, March 4, 1919.
220. *New York Times*, February 20, 1919.
221. Tuttle, Jr., *Race Riot*, pg. 19.
222. *New York Times*, May 3, 1919.
223. *Chicago Defender*, May 20, 1919.
224. Tuttle, Jr., *Race Riot*, pg. 19.
225. *New York Times*, May 3, 1919.
226. Ibid., November 19, 1919, pg. 12.
227. Ibid., April 26, 1919, Ftpg.
228. Ibid., May 7, 1919, pg. 7.

229. Ibid., June 3, 1919, Ftpg.
230. Robert K Murray, *The Red Scare: A Study in National Hysteria, 1919-1920*, pp. 58-66.
231. *New York Times*, June 3, 1919, Ftpg.
232. Ibid., June 3, 1919, Ftpg.
233. Feuerlicht, *America's Reign of Terror*, pg. 82.
234. "The Navy And The Reds," *The Fleet Review*, X (January, 1919), pg.21.
235. *New York Times*, July 5, 1919, pg. 16.
236. Ibid., July 5, 1919, Editorial Page.
237. Ibid., January 8, 1919, pg. 3.
238. Hoover, *Master of Deceit*, pg. 55.
239. *New York Times*, November 9, 1919, Ftpg.
240. Feuerlicht, *America's Reign*, pg. 87.
241. *New York Times*, January 5, 1920 headlines: "Red Concentration Camp Here Urged." Ftpg.
242. Henrickson, *Detroit Perspectives*, Interview, pp. 304-314.
243. Ibid., pg. 314.
244. *The Cleveland News*, January 6, 1920, Ftpg.
245. Hoover, *Master of Deceit*, pg. 60.
246. Halliday, *The Ignorant Armies*, pp. 23-24.
247. Ibid., pg. 218.
248. Arthur S. Link, *Woodrow Wilson and a Revolutionary World,1913-1921*, pg. 77.
249. George F. Kennan, *The Decision to Intervene*, pp. 419-420.
250. Kennan, *The Decision to Intervene*, pg. 421.
251. Robert J. Maddox, *The Unknown War With Russia*, pp. 137 & 138.
252. Pershing, John J., *My Experiences In The World War*, Vol II, pp. 176-179.
253. William S. Graves, *America's Siberian Adventure 1918-1920*, pg. 347.
254. Graves, *America's Siberian Adventure*, pg. 346.
255. Kolb, "The Bolo War," pp. 70-80; Lt. Cudahy writings.
256. Halliday, *The Ignorant Armies*, pg. Xvi.
257. Pipes, Richard, *Russia Under The Bolshevik Regime*, pg. 63.
258. Frederick Palmer, *Newton D. Baker: America at War*, 2 vols., 2:319.
259. Arkins Collection, Bentley Library, U/M.
260. David Lloyd George, *Memoirs of the Peace Conference*, pg. 251.
261. George, *Memoirs of the Peace Conference*, pg. 208.
262. Halliday, *The Ignorant Armies*, pg. 218.
263. Volkogonov, Dmitri, *Lenin, A New Biography*, pp. xxiv-xxxix.
264. *U.S. News & World Report*, November 20, 1989, "All Present and Accounted For."
265. Richard Pipes, *Russia Under the Bolshevik Regime*, pp. 68-72.
266. Robert Conquest, "The New York Review," review of Richard Pipes' *Russia Under the Bolshevik Regime*.
267. David R. Francis, *Russia From The American Embassy*, pg. 341.
268. Kennan, *Soviet-American Relation, 1917-1920*, 2:364.
269. Foreign Relations papers of the United States, 1918, 2:477-484.
270. Classified documents dated August 20, 1919, declassified September 27, 1958. H. S. Martin, Captain, U.S. Army, American Military Mission, sent to General Richardson.
271. Letter dated July 1918 to family of John Dalian. Interview with family.

272. Diary of Edwin L. Arkins, 1918-1919. Bentley Library, University of Michigan.
273. Gordon W. Smith, "Waging War in Frozen Hell: A Record of Personal Experiences." *Current History* (April 1930), pg. 70.
274. From collection of letters of Rodger Sherman Clark. Bentley Library.
275. *Chicago Sunday Tribune*, February 26, 1919. Interview with Mr. Richard Patching, July 21, 1995.
276. Interview with Mr. Ed Karkou, one of the last "Polar Bears," July 6, 1995 at his home in Pontiac Michigan. He will be 100 years old in December. He lives alone in a large home that he manages himself. He is very active and has the appearance of a 70 year old.
277. Interview with Mr. Richard Patching, July 21, 1995. His father was a "Polar Bear."
278. Interview with Mr. & Mrs. Stevenson, July 6, 1995. Her father was Lawrence Simpson, a "Polar Bear."
279. Interview with Sue Saunders, July 7, 1995. Her uncle was Sergeant Edward P. Trombley, a "Polar Bear."
280. Interview with Mr. Dalian, June 21, 1995. His father was John Dalian, a "Polar Bear."
281. From collection of letters of George Albers, 1918-1919, 40-45. Bentley Library.
282. Richard K. Kolb, "The Bolo War," *Army*, April 1988, pg. 71.
283. Christopher Lasch, *The American Liberals and the Russian Revolution*, pg. 194.
284. Andrew Soutar, *With Ironside in North Russia*, pg. 220.
285. Official documents by C.T. Williams, Deputy Commissioner, American Red Cross Mission to Russia, February 22, 1919, M & S Archives.
286. Moore, *American Expedition Fighting the Bolsheviki*, pp. 44-45.
287. Pershing, *My Experiences in the World War* Volume II and *Final Report of General John J. Pershing, Commander-In-Chief, American Expeditionary Forces* (Washington, D. C.: Government Printing Office, 1920), Pg. 55.
288. George F. Kennan, *Soviet Foreign Policy, 1917-1941*, pp. 29-30.
289. Kennan, *The Decision to Intervene*, pg. 421.
290. Halliday, *The Ignorant Armies*, pg. 218.
291. Ibid., pp. xv-xvi.
292. Louis Fischer, *The Soviets in World Affairs: A History of Relations Between the Soviet Union and the Rest of the World*, pp. 151-162.
293. D.F. Flemming, *The Cold War and Its Origins, 1917-1960*, Vol I, pp. 32-35.
294. Halliday, *The Ignorant Armies*, pg. xv.
295. E. M. Halliday, "Where Ignorant Armies Clashed by Night," *American Heritage*, 10:1, pg. 125.
296. W. P. Richardson, "America's War in Nothern Russia." *Current History* Vol. 13, pg. 289.
297. George F. Kennan, "Soviet Historiography and America's Role in the Intervention," *American Historical Review*, 55:2 (January 1960), pp. 303-304.
298. Kennan, *The Decision to Intervene*., pg. 418.
299. Ibid., pg. 421.
300. Halliday, *The Ignorant Armies*, pg. 209.
301. Interview, Mead.
302. Interview, Saunders.

303. Letter to me dated 11-7-95. Also conversation on Memorial Day, 1995 at the "Polar Bear" monument, Troy, Michigan.

304. *VFW*, "Polar Bears Vs. Bolos," Richard K. Kolb, January 1919.

305. Bozich, *Detroit's Own*, pg. 106.

306. Ibid.

307. Ibid., pg. 107.

308. Ibid., pg. 108.

309. Ibid., pp. 112-113.

310. Halliday, *The Ignorant Armies*, pg. 212.

311. Ibid., pg. 212.

312. Kolb, *Army*, "The Bolo War," April 1988, pg. 80.

313. Holliday, *The Ignorant Armies*, pg. 215. There were two groups sent - Five from the "Polar Bear" Post #436 and a separate group from the Federal Graves Registrations.

314. Walter Dundon Reminiscences, 1929-1969, Bentley Library, U/M.

315. Holliday, *The Ignorant Armies*, pg. 217.

316. Interview with Stan Bozich, January 2, 1996.

317. *Detroit Free Press*, April 7, 1985, pg. 6G.

318. Richard Hofstadter, *The American Republic*, Vol 2, pg. 370.

319. Hofstadter, *The American Republic*, Vol 2, pg. 370.

320. Colburn, Interview.

321. Kennan, *The Decision To Intervene*, pp. 482-485.

322. From archives given me by Mr. & Mrs. Stevenson (Lawrence Simpson).

✳

BIBLIOGRAPHY

Baker, Ray Stannard. *Woodrow Wilson: Life and Letters*, 8 Vols. New York:Greenwood Press, 1968.

Bechtel, Marilyn. *Six Decades That Changed The World: The U.S.S.R. After 60 Years*, New York:NWR Publications, Inc., 1978.

Bradley, John. *Allied Intervention in Russia*. New York:Basic Books, Inc., 1968.

Bozich, Stanley J. *Detroit's Own Polar Bears*. Frankenmuth, Michigan:Polar Bear Publishing Co., 1985.

Carmichael, Joel. *A Short History of the Russian Revolution*. New York:Basic Books, 1964.

Conot, Robert. *American Odyssey, A Unique History of America Told Through the Life of a Great City*. New York:William Morrow & Company, Inc., 1974.

Dobson, Christopher. *The Day They Almost Bombed Moscow*. New York: Atheneum, 1986.

Dos Passos, John. *Mr. Wilson's War*. Garden City, New York:Doubleday and Company, Inc., 1962.

Feuerlicht, Robert S. *America's Reign of Terror*. New York:Doubleday and Company, Inc., 1972.

Fischer, Louis. *The Soviets in World Affairs: A History of Relations Between the Soviet Union and the Rest of the World, 1917-1929*. New York: VintageBooks, 1951.

Flemming, D.F. *The Cold War and Its Origins, 1917-1960*. 2 Vols. New York:Doubleday and Company, 1961.

Francis, David R. *Russia From the American Embassy, 1916-1918*. New York:Charles Scribner's Sons, 1921; reprint, New York:Arno Press and *New York Times*, 1970.

Gordon, Dennis. *Quartered In Hell-The Story of American North Russian Expeditionary Force, 1918-1919*. Missoula, Montana:The Doughboy Historical Society, 1982.

157

Graves, William S. *America's Siberian Adventure: 1918-1920*. New York:Peter Smith Publishers, 1931.

Haimson, Leopold H. *The Russian Marxists and The Origins of Bolshevism*. Cambridge, Massachusetts:Harvard University Press, 1955.

Halliday, E.M. *The Ignorant Armies*. New York:Harper & Brothers, 1960.

Henrickson, Wilma. *Detroit Perspectives, Crossroads and Turning Points*. Detroit: Wayne State University Press, 1991.

Hofstadter, Richard. *The American Republic*. Volume Two. Englewood Cliffs, New Jersey:Prentice-Hall, Inc., 1970.

Hoover, J. E., *Masters of Deceit*. New York:Harper & Brothers, 1962.

Hoyt, Edwin P. *America's Wars & Military Excursions*. New York:McGraw-Hill Book Company, 1987.

Kennan, George F. *Soviet Foreign Policy, 1917-1920*. 2 Vols. New York:Atheneum, 1967.

----------. *Russia and the West Under Lenin and Stalin*. Boston:Little, Brown and Company, 1960.

----------. *The Decision to Intervene*, Vol. II. Princeton, New Jersey: Princeton University Press, 1958.

Lasch, Christopher. *The American Liberals and the Russian Revolution*. NewYork: Columbia University Press, 1962.

Link, Arthur S. *Woodrow Wilson and a Revolutionary World, 1913-1921*. Chapel Hill:University of North Carolina Press, 1982.

Lloyd George, David. *Memoirs of the Peace Conference*. 2 Vols. New Haven:Yale University Press, 1939.

MacLaren, Roy. *Canadians in Russia, 1918-1919*. Toronto: Macmilllan of Canada, 1976.

Maddox, Robert J. *The Unknown War With Russia*. San Rafael, California:Presidio Press, 1977.

McKinley, Silas Bent. *Woodrow Wilson*. New York:Frederick A. Praeger Publishers, 1957.

Moore, J. R., Mead, H. H., Jahns, L. E. The American Expedition Fighting the Bolsheviki. Detroit: Polar Bear Publishing Company, 1920.

Moorehead, Alan. *The Russian Revolution.* New York:Bantam Books, 1959.

Murray, Robert K. *The Red Scare: A Study in National Hysteria.* New York:Harper Brothers, 1965.

Palmer, Frederick. *Newton D. Baker: America at War.* 2 Vols. New York:Dodd, Meade and Company, 1931.

Pershing, John J. *My Experiences In The World War Volume II.* 1931. Reprint, NewYork:Harper & Row Publishing, Inc., Military Classics Series, 1989.

Pipes, Richard. *Russia Under the Bolshevik Regime.* New York:Alfred A. Knopf,1993.

----------. *The Russian Revolution.* New York:Alfred A. Knopf, 1990.

Rubenstein, Bruce A. *Michigan – A History Of The Great Lakes State.* Wheeling, Illinois:Harlan Davidson, Inc., 1995.

Soutar, Andrew. *With Ironside in North Russia.* London:Hutchinson and Company, 1940; reprint, New York:Arno Press, 1970.

Tuttle, Willilam M. Jr. *Race Riot, Chicago in the Red Summer of 1919.* New York:Atheneum, 1970.

Ulam, Adam B. *Expansion and Coexistence: The History of Soviet Foreign Policy,1917-1967.* New York:Praeger Publishers, 1968.

Ullman, Richard H. *Intervention and the War.* Princeton, New Jersey:Princeton University Press, 1961.

Unterberger, Betty M. *America's Siberian Expedition, 1918-1920: A Study of National Policy.* Durham, North Carolina:Duke University Press, 1956.

Volkogonov, Dmitri. *Lenin, A New Biography.* New York:The Free Press, 1994.

Weeks, Albert L. *The First Bolshevik.* New York:New York University Press, London:University of London Press Limited, 1968.

Wheeler-Bennett, John W. *Brest-Litovsk, The Forgotten Peace March 1918.* New York:The Norton Library, 1971.

Woodford, Frank & Arthur. *All Our Yesterdays, A Brief History of Detroit*. Detroit: Wayne State University Press, 1969.

Consulted

Angarsky, Andrew. *Eighty-Seven Days*. New York:Alfred A. Knopf, 1963.

Crankshaw, Edward. *The Shadow of the Winter Palace, The Drift To Revolution 1825-1917*. Penguin Books, 1976.

Dziewanowski, M.K. *A History of Soviet Russia*. New Jersey:Prentice Hall,1989.

Foglesong, David S. *America's Secret War Against Bolshevism*. Chapel Hill:The University of North Carolina Press, 1995.

Gregory, Ross. *The Origins of American Intervention in the First World War*. New York:W.W. Norton & Company, Inc., 1971.

Knock, Thomas J. *To End All Wars*. Princeton, New Jersey:Princeton University Press, 1992.

Lee, Dwight E. *The Outbreak of the First World War, Who Was Responsible?* Boston:D. C. Heath and Company, 1958.

Lochbiler, Don. *Detroit's Coming of Age, 1873 to 1973*. Detroit:A Savoyard Book published by Wayne State University Press, 1973.

Massie, Robert K. *Nicholas and Alexandra*. A Dell Book, 1969.

Takaki, Ronald. *A Different Mirror, A History of Multicultural America*. Boston:Little, Brown and Company, 1993.

Walicki, Andrazej. *A History of Russian Thought, From the Enlightenment to Marxism*. Stanford, California:Stanford University Press, 1979.

Weidle, Wladimir. *Russia: Absent and Present*. New York:Vintage Books, 1961.

Widick, B.J. *Detroit, City of Race and Class Violence*. Chicago:Quadranagle Books, 1972.

Newspapers

The Cleveland News, January 6, 1920.
The Chicago Daily Tribune, February 10,1919.
The Chicago Sunday Tribune, February 26, 1919.
Chicago Defender, May 20, 1919.
The Detroit Free Press, February 2, 1919.
The Detroit Free Press, February 4, 1919.
The Detroit Free Press, February 6, 1919.
The Detroit Free Press, February 12, 1919.
The Detroit Free Press, February 13, 1919.
The Detroit Free Press, February 14, 1919.
The Detroit Free Press, February 15, 1919.
The Detroit Free Press, February 22, 1919.
The Detroit Free Press, May 1, 1919.
The Detroit Free Press, May 24, 1919.
The Detroit Free Press,April 7, 1985.
The Detroit Journal, February 17, 1919.
The Detroit Journal,February 19,1919.
The Detroit Journal, April 4, 1919.
The Detroit News, January 12, 1919.
The Detroit News, January 29, 1919.
The Detroit News, January 31, 1919.
The Detroit News, February 1, 1919.
The Detroit News, February 3, 1919.
The Detroit News, February 5, 1919.
The Detroit News, February 6, 1919.
The Detroit News, February 12, 1919.
The Detroit News, February 13, 1919
The Detroit News, February 14, 1919..
The Detroit News, February 15, 1919.
The Detroit News, February 17, 1919.
The Detroit News, February 18, 1919.
The Detroit News, February 20, 1919.
The Detroit News, April 5, 1919.
New York Times, January 6, 1919.
New York Times, January 8, 1919.
New York Times, January 13, 1919.
New York Times, January 19, 1919.
New York Times, January 20, 1919.
New York Times, February 9, 1919.
New York Times, February 13, 1919.
New York Times, February 14, 1919.

New York Times, February 18, 1919.
New York Times, February 20, 1919.
New York Times, February 27, 1919.
New York Times, March 4, 1919.
New York Times, March 16, 1919.
New York Times, April 26, 1919.
New York Times, May 3, 1919.
New York Times, May 7, 1919.
New York Times, June 3, 1919.
New York Times, July 5, 1919.
New York Times, November 8, 1919.
New York Times, November 9, 1919.
New York Times, November 19, 1919.
New York Times, December 1, 1919.
New York Times, January 5, 1920.
The Sunday Cleveland Leader, July 7, 1918.
Syracuse Post-Standard, July 29, 1919.

Magazines, Documents and Interviews

Army, April 1988.
Current History, February 1921.
Current History, April 1930.
Literary Digest, July 12, 1919.
Michigan History, May/June 1988.
U.S. News & World Report, November 13, 1995.
VFW, January 1988.

Papers Relating to the Foreign Relations of the United States, 1917, 1918, 1919, Russia. United States Department of State, three vols., Washington D.C.

V.I. Lenin: Collected Works, Alexander Trachtenberg. 45 Vols. New York: International Publication, 1945.

Letters, manuscripts and diaries from the Bentley Library, University of Michigan and the Archives from The Military and Space Museum in Frankenmuth, Michigan.

Interview, Stanley Bozich. Numerous occasions between 1994-1996.

Interview, Cleo Colburn, Polar Bear. February 17, 1992.

Interview, Mr. Dalian. Father John Dalian, Polar Bear, June 21, 1995.

Interview, Mr. Ed Karkau, Polar Bear. July 6, 1995.

Interview, Mr. Hudson Mead. Father Harry Mead, Polar Bear, July 13, 1995.

Interview, Mr. Richard Patching. Father was a Polar Bear, July 21, 1995.

Interview, Mr. Gregg Ponke. Grandfather Lawrence Simpson, Polar Bear, November 7, 1995.

Interview, Ms. Sue Saunders. Uncle Edward P. Trombley, Polar Bear, July 7, 1995.

Interview Mr. & Mrs. Stevenson. Mrs. Stevenson's father Lawrence Simpson, Polar Bear, July 6, 1995

INDEX

✳